PENGUIN PLAYS

LOOK BACK IN ANGER

John Osborne was born in London in 1929 and began work as a reporter before becoming an actor. *Look Back in Anger*, which in effect set off a whole revival of British drama and helped to give currency to the phrase "angry young man" in reference to certain British writers of the 1950s, was first performed in the opening season of the English Stage Company at the Royal Court Theatre in 1956 and subsequently on Broadway in 1957. Since then Mr. Osborne has written over thirty stage and television plays, including *The Entertainer*, starring Sir Laurence Olivier, *Luther*, starring Albert Finney, *Inadmissible Evidence*, starring Nicol Williamson, *A Patriot for Me*, starring Maximilian Schell, *A Sense of Detachment, West of Suez, Watch It Come Down*, and, most recently, *Dejavu*, a sequel to *Look Back in Anger*. John Osborne won an Oscar for the screenplay of *Tom Jones* and has written two volumes of autobiography, *A Better Class of Person* and *Almost a Gentleman*. He lives in Shropshire, England.

Look Back in Anger

by
JOHN OSBORNE

PENGUIN BOOKS

PENGUIN BOOKS

Published by the Penguin Group
Penguin Books USA Inc.,
375 Hudson Street, New York, New York 10014, U.S.A.
Penguin Books Ltd, 27 Wrights Lane, London W8 5TZ, England
Penguin Books Australia Ltd, Ringwood, Victoria, Australia
Penguin Books Canada Ltd, 10 Alcorn Avenue,
Toronto, Ontario, Canada M4V 3B2
Penguin Books (N.Z.) Ltd, 182–190 Wairau Road, Auckland 10, New Zealand

Penguin Books Ltd, Registered Offices:
Harmondsworth, Middlesex, England

First published in the United States of America by
Criterion Books, Inc., 1957
Published in Penguin Books by arrangement with
S. G. Phillips, Inc., 1982

15   17   19   20   18   16

LIBRARY OF CONGRESS CATALOGING IN PUBLICATION DATA
Osborne, John, 1929–
Look back in anger.
Reprint. Originally published: New York:
Criterion Books, 1957.
I. Title.
PR6092.S39L6   1982   822'.914   82-9144
ISBN 0 14 048.175 3   AACR2

Printed in the United States of America
Set in Caslon

CAUTION: This play in its printed form is designed for the reading public only. All dramatic, motion picture, radio, television, and other rights in it are fully protected by copyright in the United States of America, the British Empire, including the Dominion of Canada, and all other countries of the Copyright Union. No performance, professional or amateur, nor any broadcast, nor any public reading or recitation may be given without written permission in advance. All professional inquiries in the United States and Canada should be addressed to Robert A. Freedman Dramatic Agency, Inc., 1501 Broadway, Suite 2310, New York, New York 10036. Amateur rights in the United States and Canada are controlled solely by Evans Brothers Ltd, Montague House, Russell Square, London WCrB 5BX, England, to whom application must be made for a license to perform this play *before rehearsals begin.*

For
MY FATHER

CAST
In Order of Appearance

CONTENTS

The action throughout takes place in the
Porters' one-room flat in the Midlands.

TIME: The present.

The first performance in Great Britain of LOOK BACK IN ANGER was given at the Royal Court Theatre, Sloane Square, London, on 8th May, 1956, by the English Stage Company. It was directed by Tony Richardson, and the décor was by Alan Tagg. The cast was as follows:

JIMMY PORTER	Kenneth Haigh
CLIFF LEWIS	Alan Bates
ALISON PORTER	Mary Ure
HELENA CHARLES	Helena Hughes
COLONEL REDFERN	John Welsh

ACT I

The Porters' one-room flat in a large Midland town.
Early evening. April.

The scene is a fairly large attic room, at the top of a
large Victorian house. The ceiling slopes down quite
sharply from L. to R. Down R. are two small low
windows. In front of these is a dark oak dressing table.
Most of the furniture is simple, and rather old. Up R. is
a double bed, running the length of most of the back
wall, the rest of which is taken up with a shelf of books.
Down R. below the bed is a heavy chest of drawers,
covered with books, neckties and odds and ends,
including a large, tattered toy teddy bear and soft,
woolly squirrel. Up L. is a door. Below this a small
wardrobe. Most of the wall L. is taken up with a high,
oblong window. This looks out on to the landing, but
light comes through it from a skylight beyond. Below
the wardrobe is a gas stove, and, beside this, a wooden
food cupboard, on which is a small, portable radio.
Down C. is a sturdy dining table and three chairs, and,
below this, L. and R., two deep, shabby leather
armchairs.

AT RISE OF CURTAIN, JIMMY and CLIFF are seated in the
two armchairs R. and L., respectively. All that we can
see of either of them is two pairs of legs, sprawled way
out beyond the newspapers which hide the rest of them
from sight. They are both reading. Beside them, and
between them, is a jungle of newspapers and weeklies.
When we do eventually see them, we find that JIMMY is
a tall, thin young man about twenty-five, wearing a
very worn tweed jacket and flannels. Clouds of smoke
fill the room from the pipe he is smoking. He is a
disconcerting mixture of sincerity and cheerful malice,
of tenderness and freebooting cruelty; restless,

9

importunate, full of pride, a combination which alienates the sensitive and insensitive alike. Blistering honesty, or apparent honesty, like his, makes few friends. To many he may seem sensitive to the point of vulgarity. To others, he is simply a loudmouth. To be as vehement as he is is to be almost non-committal.

CLIFF is the same age, short, dark, big boned, wearing a pullover and grey, new, but very creased trousers. He is easy and relaxed, almost to lethargy, with the rather sad, natural intelligence of the self-taught. If JIMMY alienates love, CLIFF seems to exact it—demonstrations of it, at least, even from the cautious. He is a soothing, natural counterpoint to JIMMY.

Standing L., below the food cupboard, is ALISON. She is leaning over an ironing board. Beside her is a pile of clothes. Hers is the most elusive personality to catch in the uneasy polyphony of these three people. She is turned in a different key, a key of well-bred malaise that is often drowned in the robust orchestration of the other two. Hanging over the grubby, but expensive, skirt she is wearing is a cherry red shirt of JIMMY'S, but she manages somehow to look quite elegant in it. She is roughly the same age as the men. Somehow, their combined physical oddity makes her beauty more striking than it really is. She is tall, slim, dark. The bones of her face are long and delicate. There is a surprising reservation about her eyes, which are so large and deep they should make equivocation impossible. The room is still, smoke filled. The only sound is the occasional thud of ALISON'S iron on the board. It is one of those chilly Spring evenings, all cloud and shadows. Presently, JIMMY throws his paper down.

JIMMY: Why do I do this every Sunday? Even the book reviews seem to be the same as last week's. Different books—same reviews. Have you finished that one yet?

CLIFF: Not yet.

JIMMY: I've just read three whole columns on the English

Novel. Half of it's in French. Do the Sunday papers make *you* feel ignorant?

CLIFF: Not 'arf.

JIMMY: Well, you *are* ignorant. You're just a peasant. (*To Alison.*) What about you? You're not a peasant are you?

ALISON: (*absently*). What's that?

JIMMY: I said do the papers make you feel you're not so brilliant after all?

ALISON: Oh—I haven't read them yet.

JIMMY: I didn't ask you that. I said——

CLIFF: Leave the poor girlie alone. She's busy.

JIMMY: Well, she can talk, can't she? You can talk, can't you? You can express an opinion. Or does the White Woman's Burden make it impossible to think?

ALISON: I'm sorry. I wasn't listening properly.

JIMMY: You bet you weren't listening. Old Porter talks, and everyone turns over and goes to sleep. And Mrs. Porter gets 'em all going with the first yawn.

CLIFF: Leave her alone, I said.

JIMMY: (*shouting*). All right, dear. Go back to sleep. It was only me talking. You know? Talking? Remember? I'm sorry.

CLIFF: Stop yelling. I'm trying to read.

JIMMY: Why do you bother? You can't understand a word of it.

CLIFF: Uh huh.

JIMMY: You're too ignorant.

CLIFF: Yes, and uneducated. Now shut up, will you?

JIMMY: Why don't you get my wife to explain it to you? She's educated. (*To her.*) That's right, isn't it?

CLIFF: (*kicking out at him from behind his paper*). Leave her alone, I said.

JIMMY: Do that again, you Welsh ruffian, and I'll pull your ears off.

He bangs Cliff's paper out of his hands.

CLIFF: (*leaning forward*). Listen—I'm trying to better myself. Let me get on with it, you big, horrible man. Give it me. (*Puts his hand out for paper.*)

ALISON: Oh, give it to him, Jimmy, for heaven's sake! I can't think!

CLIFF: Yes, come on, give me the paper. She can't think.

JIMMY: Can't think! (*Throws the paper back at him.*) She hasn't had a thought for years! Have you?

ALISON: No.

JIMMY: (*Picks up a weekly.*) I'm getting hungry.

ALISON: Oh no, not already!

CLIFF: He's a bloody pig.

JIMMY: I'm not a pig. I just like food—that's all.

CLIFF: Like it! You're like a sexual maniac—only with you it's food. You'll end up in the *News of the World*, boyo, you wait. James Porter, aged twenty-five, was bound over last week after pleading guilty to interfering with a small cabbage and two tins of beans on his way home from the Builder's Arms. The accused said he hadn't been feeling well for some time, and had been having black-outs. He asked for his good record as an air-raid warden, second class, to be taken into account.

JIMMY: (*Grins.*) Oh, yes, yes, yes. I like to eat. I'd like to live too. Do you mind?

CLIFF: Don't see any use in your eating at all. You never get any fatter.

JIMMY: People like me don't get fat. I've tried to tell you before. We just burn everything up. Now shut up while I read. You can make me some more tea.

CLIFF: Good God, you've just had a great potful! I only had one cup.

JIMMY: Like hell! Make some more.

CLIFF: (*to Alison*). Isn't that right? Didn't I only have one cup?

ALISON: (*without looking up*). That's right.

CLIFF: There you are. And she only had one cup too. I saw her. You guzzled the lot.

JIMMY: (*reading his weekly*). Put the kettle on.

CLIFF: Put it on yourself. You've creased up my paper.

JIMMY: I'm the only one who knows how to treat a paper, or anything else, in this house. (*Picks up another paper.*) Girl here wants to know whether her boy friend will lose all respect for her if she gives him what he asks for. Stupid bitch.

CLIFF: Just let me get at her, that's all.

JIMMY: Who buys this damned thing? (*Throws it down.*) Haven't you read the other posh paper yet?

CLIFF: Which?

JIMMY: Well, there are only two posh papers on a Sunday— the one you're reading, and this one. Come on, let me have that one, and you take this.

CLIFF: Oh, all right.

They exchange.

I was only reading the Bishop of Bromley. (*Puts out his hand to Alison.*) How are you, dullin'?

ALISON: All right thank you, dear.

CLIFF: (*grasping her hand*). Why don't you leave all that, and sit down for a bit? You look tired.

ALISON: (*smiling*). I haven't much more to do.

CLIFF: (*kisses her hand, and puts her fingers in his mouth*). She's a beautiful girl, isn't she?

JIMMY: That's what they all tell me.

His eyes meet hers.

CLIFF: It's a lovely, delicious paw you've got. Ummmmm. I'm going to bite it off.

ALISON: Don't! I'll burn his shirt.

JIMMY: Give her her finger back, and don't be so sickening. What's the Bishop of Bromley say?

CLIFF: (*letting go of Alison*). Oh, it says here that he makes a very moving appeal to all Christians to do all they can to assist in the manufacture of the H-Bomb.

JIMMY: Yes, well, that's quite moving, I suppose. (*To Alison.*) Are you moved, my darling?

ALISON: Well, naturally.

JIMMY: There you are: even my wife is moved. I ought to send the Bishop a subscription. Let's see. What else does he say. Dumdidumdidumdidum. Ah yes. He's upset because someone has suggested that he supports the rich against the poor. He says he denies the difference of class distinctions. "This idea has been persistently

13

and wickedly fostered by—the working classes!" Well!
*He looks up at both of them for reaction, but Cliff is
reading, and Alison is intent on her ironing.*

JIMMY: (*to Cliff*). Did you read that bit?

CLIFF: Um?
He has lost them, and he knows it, but he won't leave it.

JIMMY: (*to Alison*). You don't suppose your father could have
written it, do you?

ALISON: Written what?

JIMMY: What I just read out, of course.

ALISON: Why should my father have written it?

JIMMY: Sounds rather like Daddy, don't you think?

ALISON: Does it?

JIMMY: Is the Bishop of Bromley his nom de plume, do you
think?

CLIFF: Don't take any notice of him. He's being offensive.
And it's so easy for him.

JIMMY: (*quickly*). Did you read about the woman who went to
the mass meeting of a certain American evangelist at
Earls Court? She went forward, to declare herself for
love or whatever it is, and, in the rush of converts to
get to the front, she broke four ribs and got kicked in
the head. She was yelling her head off in agony, but
with 50,000 people putting all they'd got into "Onward
Christian Soldiers", nobody even knew she was there.
He looks up sharply for a response, but there isn't any.
Sometimes, I wonder if there isn't something wrong
with me. What about that tea?

CLIFF: (*still behind paper*). What tea?

JIMMY: Put the kettle on.
Alison looks up at him.

ALISON: Do you want some more tea?

JIMMY: I don't know. No, I don't think so.

ALISON: Do you want some, Cliff?

JIMMY: No, he doesn't. How much longer will you be doing
that?

ALISON: Won't be long.

JIMMY: God, how I hate Sundays! It's always so depressing,

always the same. We never seem to get any further, do we? Always the same ritual. Reading the papers, drinking tea, ironing. A few more hours, and another week gone. Our youth is slipping away. Do you know that?

CLIFF: (*throws down paper*). What's that?

JIMMY: (*casually*). Oh, nothing, nothing. Damn you, damn both of you, damn them all.

CLIFF: Let's go to the pictures. (*To Alison.*) What do you say, lovely?

ALISON: I don't think I'll be able to. Perhaps Jimmy would like to go. (*To Jimmy.*) Would you like to?

JIMMY: And have my enjoyment ruined by the Sunday night yobs in the front row? No, thank you. (*Pause.*) Did you read Priestley's piece this week? Why on earth I ask, I don't know. I know damned well you haven't. Why do I spend ninepence on that damned paper every week? Nobody reads it except me. Nobody can be bothered. No one can raise themselves out of their delicious sloth. You two will drive me round the bend soon—I know it, as sure as I'm sitting here. I know you're going to drive me mad. Oh heavens, how I long for a little ordinary human enthusiasm. Just enthusiasm —that's all. I want to hear a warm, thrilling voice cry out Hallelujah! (*He bangs his breast theatrically.*) Hallelujah! I'm alive! I've an idea. Why don't we have a little game? Let's pretend that we're human beings, and that we're actually alive. Just for a while. What do you say? Let's pretend we're human. (*He looks from one to the other.*) Oh, brother, it's such a long time since I was with anyone who got enthusiastic about anything.

CLIFF: What did he say?

JIMMY: (*resentful of being dragged away from his pursuit of Alison*). What did who say?

CLIFF: Mr. Priestley.

JIMMY: What he always says, I suppose. He's like Daddy— still casting well-fed glances back to the Edwardian twilight from his comfortable, disenfranchised wilderness. What the devil have you done to those trousers?

CLIFF: Done?

JIMMY: Are they the ones you bought last week-end? Look at them. Do you see what he's done to those new trousers?

ALISON: You are naughty, Cliff. They look dreadful.

JIMMY: You spend good money on a new pair of trousers, and then sprawl about in them like a savage. What do you think you're going to do when I'm not around to look after you? Well, what are you going to do? Tell me?

CLIFF: (*grinning*). I don't know. (*To Alison.*) What am I going to do, lovely?

ALISON: You'd better take them off.

JIMMY: Yes, go on. Take 'em off. And I'll kick your behind for you.

ALISON: I'll give them a press while I've got the iron on.

CLIFF: O.K. (*Starts taking them off.*) I'll just empty the pockets. (*Takes out keys, matches, handkerchief.*)

JIMMY: Give me those matches, will you?

CLIFF: Oh, you're not going to start up that old pipe again, are you? It stinks the place out. (*To Alison.*) Doesn't it smell awful?

Jimmy grabs the matches, and lights up.

ALISON: I don't mind it. I've got used to it.

JIMMY: She's a great one for getting used to things. If she were to die, and wake up in paradise—after the first five minutes, she'd have got used to it.

CLIFF: (*hands her the trousers*). Thank you, lovely. Give me a cigarette, will you?

JIMMY: Don't give him one.

CLIFF: I can't stand the stink of that old pipe any longer. I must have a cigarette.

JIMMY: I thought the doctor said no cigarettes?

CLIFF: Oh, why doesn't he shut up?

JIMMY: All right. They're your ulcers. Go ahead, and have a bellyache, if that's what you want. I give up. I give up. I'm sick of doing things for people. And all for what?

16

Alison gives Cliff a cigarette. They both light up, and she goes on with her ironing.

Nobody thinks, nobody cares. No beliefs, no convictions and no enthusiasm. Just another Sunday evening.

Cliff sits down again, in his pullover and shorts.

Perhaps there's a concert on. (*Picks up* Radio Times) Ah. (*Nudges Cliff with his foot.*) Make some more tea.

Cliff grunts. He is reading again.

Oh, yes. There's a Vaughan Williams. Well, that's something, anyway. Something strong, something simple, something English. I suppose people like me aren't supposed to be very patriotic. Somebody said— what was it—we get our cooking from Paris (that's a laugh), our politics from Moscow, and our morals from Port Said. Something like that, anyway. Who was it? (*Pause.*) Well, you wouldn't know anyway. I hate to admit it, but I think I can understand how her Daddy must have felt when he came back from India, after all those years away. The old Edwardian brigade do make their brief little world look pretty tempting. All home-made cakes and croquet, bright ideas, bright uniforms. Always the same picture: high summer, the long days in the sun, slim volumes of verse, crisp linen, the smell of starch. What a romantic picture. Phoney too, of course. It must have rained sometimes. Still, even I regret it somehow, phoney or not. If you've no world of your own, it's rather pleasant to regret the passing of someone else's. I must be getting sentimental. But I must say it's pretty dreary living in the American Age—unless you're an American of course. Perhaps all our children will be Americans. That's a thought isn't it?

He gives Cliff a kick, and shouts at him.

I said that's a thought!

CLIFF: You did?

JIMMY: You sit there like a lump of dough. I thought you were going to make me some tea.

Cliff groans. Jimmy turns to Alison.

Is your friend Webster coming tonight?

ALISON: He might drop in. You know what he is.

JIMMY: Well, I hope he doesn't. I don't think I could take Webster tonight.

ALISON: I thought you said he was the only person who spoke your language.

JIMMY: So he is. Different dialect but same language. I like him. He's got bite, edge, drive——

ALISON: Enthusiasm.

JIMMY: You've got it. When he comes here, I begin to feel exhilarated. He doesn't like me, but he gives me something, which is more than I get from most people. Not since——

ALISON: Yes, we know. Not since you were living with Madeline. *She folds some of the clothes she has already ironed, and crosses to the bed with them.*

CLIFF: (*behind paper again*). Who's Madeline?

ALISON: Oh, wake up, dear. You've heard about Madeline enough times. She was his mistress. Remember? When he was fourteen. Or was it thirteen?

JIMMY: Eighteen.

ALISON: He owes just about everything to Madeline.

CLIFF: I get mixed up with all your women. Was she the one all those years older than you?

JIMMY: Ten years.

CLIFF: Proper little Marchbanks, you are!

JIMMY: What time's that concert on? (*Checks paper.*)

CLIFF: (*yawns*). Oh, I feel so sleepy. Don't feel like standing behind that blinking sweet-stall again tomorrow. Why don't you do it on your own, and let me sleep in?

JIMMY: I've got to be at the factory first thing, to get some more stock, so you'll have to put it up on your own. Another five minutes.
Alison has returned to her ironing board. She stands with her arms folded, smoking, staring thoughtfully.
She had more animation in her little finger than you two put together.

CLIFF: Who did?

ALISON: Madeline.

JIMMY: Her curiosity about things, and about people was staggering. It wasn't just a naïve nosiness. With her, it was simply the delight of being awake, and watching. *Alison starts to press Cliff's trousers.*

CLIFF: (*behind paper*). Perhaps I will make some tea, after all.

JIMMY: (*quietly*). Just to be with her was an adventure. Even to sit on the top of a bus with her was like setting out with Ulysses.

CLIFF: Wouldn't have said Webster was much like Ulysses. He's an ugly little devil.

JIMMY: I'm not talking about Webster, stupid. He's all right though, in his way. A sort of female Emily Brontë. He's the only one of your friends (*to Alison*) who's worth tuppence, anyway. I'm surprised you get on with him.

ALISON: So is he, I think.

JIMMY: (*rising to window R., and looking out*). He's not only got guts, but sensitivity as well. That's about the rarest combination I can think of. None of your other friends have got either.

ALISON: (*very quietly and earnestly*). Jimmy, please—don't go on. *He turns and looks at her. The tired appeal in her voice has pulled him up suddenly. But he soon gathers himself for a new assault. He walks C., behind Cliff, and stands, looking down at his head.*

JIMMY: Your friends—there's a shower for you.

CLIFF: (*mumbling*). Dry up. Let her get on with my trousers.

JIMMY: (*musingly*). Don't think I could provoke her. Nothing I could do would provoke her. Not even if I were to drop dead.

CLIFF: Then drop dead.

JIMMY: They're either militant like her Mummy and Daddy. Militant, arrogant and full of malice. Or vague. She's somewhere between the two.

CLIFF: Why don't you listen to that concert of yours? And don't stand behind me. That blooming droning on behind me gives me a funny feeling down the spine.

19

Jimmy gives his ears a twist and Cliff roars with pain.
Jimmy grins back at him.

That hurt, you rotten sadist! (*To Alison.*) I wish you'd
kick his head in for him.

JIMMY: (*moving in between them*). Have you ever seen her
brother? Brother Nigel? The straight-backed, chinless
wonder from Sandhurst? I only met him once myself.
He asked me to step outside when I told his mother
she was evil minded.

CLIFF: And did you?

JIMMY: Certainly not. He's a big chap. Well, you've never
heard so many well-bred commonplaces come from
beneath the same bowler hat. The Platitude from
Outer Space—that's brother Nigel. He'll end up in the
Cabinet one day, make no mistake. But somewhere at
the back of that mind is the vague knowledge that he
and his pals have been plundering and fooling
everybody for generations. (*Going upstage, and turning.*)
Now Nigel is just about as vague as you can get
without being actually invisible. And invisible
politicians aren't much use to anyone—not even to *his*
supporters! And nothing is more vague about Nigel
than his knowledge. His knowledge of life and
ordinary human beings is so hazy, he really deserves
some sort of decoration for it—a medal inscribed
"For Vaguery in the Field". But it wouldn't do for him
to be troubled by any stabs of conscience, however
vague. (*Moving down again.*) Besides, he's a patriot and
an Englishman, and he doesn't like the idea that he may
have been selling out his countryman all these years, so
what does he do? The only thing he *can* do—seek
sanctuary in his own stupidity. The only way to keep
things as much like they always have been as possible, is
to make any alternative too much for your poor, tiny
brain to grasp. It takes some doing nowadays. It really
does. But they knew all about character building at
Nigel's school, and he'll make it all right. Don't you

worry, he'll make it. And, what's more, he'll do it better than anybody else!

There is no sound, only the plod of Alison's iron. Her eyes are fixed on what she is doing. Cliff stares at the floor. His cheerfulness has deserted him for the moment. Jimmy is rather shakily triumphant. He cannot allow himself to look at either of them to catch their response to his rhetoric, so he moves across to the window, to recover himself, and look out.

It's started to rain. That's all it needs. This room and the rain.

He's been cheated out of his response, but he's got to draw blood somehow.

(*conversationally*). Yes, that's the little woman's family. You know Mummy and Daddy, of course. And don't let the Marquess of Queensberry manner fool you. They'll kick you in the groin while you're handing your hat to the maid. As for Nigel and Alison——(*In a reverent, Stuart Hibberd voice.*) Nigel and Alison. They're what they sound like: sycophantic, phlegmatic and pusillanimous.

CLIFF: I'll bet that concert's started by now. Shall I put it on?

JIMMY: I looked up that word the other day. It's one of those words I've never been quite sure of, but always thought I knew.

CLIFF: What was that?

JIMMY: I told you—pusillanimous. Do you know what it means?

Cliff shakes his head.

Neither did I really. All this time, I have been married to this woman, this monument to non-attachment, and suddenly I discover that there is actually a word that sums her up. Not just an adjective in the English language to describe her with—it's her name! Pusillanimous! It sounds like some fleshy Roman matron, doesn't it? The Lady Pusillanimous seen here with her husband Sextus, on their way to the Games.

Cliff looks troubled, and glances uneasily at Alison.

Poor old Sextus! If he were put into a Hollywood
film, he's so unimpressive, they'd make some poor
British actor play the part. He doesn't know it, but
those beefcake Christians will make off with his wife
in the wonder of stereophonic sound before the picture's
over.
Alison leans against the board, and closes her eyes.
The Lady Pusillanimous has been promised a brighter
easier world than old Sextus can ever offer her. Hi,
Pusey! What say we get the hell down to the Arena,
and maybe feed ourselves to a couple of lions, huh?

ALISON: God help me, if he doesn't stop, I'll go out of my
mind in a minute.

JIMMY: Why don't you? That would be something, anyway.
(*Crosses to chest of drawers R.*) But I haven't told you
what it means yet, have I? (*Picks up dictionary.*) I don't
have to tell her—she knows. In fact, if my
pronunciation is at fault, she'll probably wait for a
suitably public moment to correct it. Here it is. I
quote: Pusillanimous. Adjective. Wanting of firmness
of mind, of small courage, having a little mind, mean
spirited, cowardly, timid of mind. From the Latin
pusillus, very little, and animus, the mind. (*Slams the
book shut.*) That's my wife! That's *her* isn't it?
Behold the Lady Pusillanimous. (*Shouting hoarsely.*)
Hi, Pusey! When's your next picture?
*Jimmy watches her, waiting for her to break. For no
more than a flash, Alison's face seems to contort, and it
looks as though she might throw her head back, and
scream. But it passes in a moment. She is used to these
carefully rehearsed attacks, and it doesn't look as though
he will get his triumph tonight. She carries on with her
ironing. Jimmy crosses, and switches on the radio. The
Vaughan Williams concert has started. He goes back to
his chair, leans back in it, and closes his eyes.*

ALISON: (*handing Cliff his trousers*). There you are, dear. They're
not very good, but they'll do for now.
Cliff gets up and puts them on.

22

CLIFF: Oh, that's lovely.

ALISON: Now try and look after them. I'll give them a real press later on.

CLIFF: Thank you, you beautiful, darling girl.

He puts his arms round her waist, and kisses her. She smiles, and gives his nose a tug. Jimmy watches from his chair.

ALISON: *(to Cliff).* Let's have a cigarette, shall we?

CLIFF: That's a good idea. Where are they?

ALISON: On the stove. Do you want one Jimmy?

JIMMY: No thank you, I'm trying to listen. Do you mind?

CLIFF: Sorry, your lordship.

He puts a cigarette in Alison's mouth, and one in his own, and lights up. Cliff sits down, and picks up his paper. Alison goes back to her board. Cliff throws down paper, picks up another, and thumbs through that.

JIMMY: Do you have to make all that racket?

CLIFF: Oh, sorry.

JIMMY: It's quite a simple thing, you know—turning over a page. Anyway, that's my paper. *(Snatches it away.)*

CLIFF: Oh, don't be so mean!

JIMMY: Price ninepence, obtainable from any newsagent's. Now let me hear the music, for God's sake.

Pause.

(to Alison). Are you going to be much longer doing that?

ALISON: Why?

JIMMY: Perhaps you haven't noticed it, but it's interfering with the radio.

ALISON: I'm sorry. I shan't be much longer.

A pause. The iron mingles with the music. Cliff shifts restlessly in his chair, Jimmy watches Alison, his foot beginning to twitch dangerously. Presently, he gets up quickly, crossing below Alison to the radio, and turns it off. What did you do that for?

JIMMY: I wanted to listen to the concert, that's all.

ALISON: Well, what's stopping you?

JIMMY: Everyone's making such a din—that's what's stopping me.

ALISON: Well, I'm very sorry, but I can't just stop everything because you want to listen to music.

JIMMY: Why not?

ALISON: Really, Jimmy, you're like a child.

JIMMY: Don't try and patronise me. (*Turning to Cliff.*) She's so clumsy. I watch for her to do the same things every night. The way she jumps on the bed, as if she were stamping on someone's face, and draws the curtains back with a great clatter, in that casually destructive way of hers. It's like someone launching a battleship. Have you ever noticed how noisy women are? (*Crosses below chairs to L.C.*) Have you? The way they kick the floor about, simply walking over it? Or have you watched them sitting at their dressing tables, dropping their weapons and banging down their bits of boxes and brushes and lipsticks?

He faces her dressing table.

I've watched her doing it night after night. When you see a woman in front of her bedroom mirror, you realise what a refined sort of a butcher she is. (*Turns in.*) Did you ever see some dirty old Arab, sticking his fingers into some mess of lamb fat and gristle? Well, she's just like that. Thank God they don't have many women surgeons! Those primitive hands would have your guts out in no time. Flip! Out it comes, like the powder out of its box. Flop! Back it goes, like the powder puff on the table.

CLIFF: (*grimacing cheerfully*). Ugh! Stop it!

JIMMY: (*moving upstage*). She'd drop your guts like hair clips and fluff all over the floor. You've got to be fundamentally insensitive to be as noisy and as clumsy as that.

He moves C., and leans against the table.

I had a flat underneath a couple of girls once. You heard every damned thing those bastards did, all day and night. The most simple, everyday actions were a sort of assault course on your sensibilities. I used to plead with them. I even got to screaming the most

24

ingenious obscenities I could think of, up the stairs at them. But nothing, nothing, would move them. With those two, even a simple visit to the lavatory sounded like a medieval siege. Oh, they beat me in the end—I had to go. I expect they're still at it. Or they're probably married by now, and driving some other poor devils out of their minds. Slamming their doors, stamping their high heels, banging their irons and saucepans—the eternal flaming racket of the female.
Church bells start ringing outside.

JIMMY: Oh, hell! Now the bloody bells have started!
He rushes to the window.
Wrap it up, will you? Stop ringing those bells! There's somebody going crazy in here! I don't want to hear them!

ALISON: Stop shouting! (*Recovering immediately.*) You'll have Miss Drury up here.

JIMMY: I don't give a damn about Miss Drury—that mild old gentlewoman doesn't fool me, even if she takes in you two. She's an old robber. She gets more than enough out of us for this place every week. Anyway, she's probably in church, (*points to the window*) swinging on those bloody bells!

Cliff goes to the window, and closes it.

CLIFF: Come on now, be a good boy. I'll take us all out, and we'll have a drink.

JIMMY: They're not open yet. It's Sunday. Remember? Anyway, it's raining.

CLIFF: Well, shall we dance?
He pushes Jimmy round the floor, who is past the mood for this kind of fooling.
Do you come here often?

JIMMY: Only in the mating season. All right, all right, very funny.
He tries to escape, but Cliff holds him like a vice.
Let me go.

CLIFF: Not until you've apologised for being nasty to everyone. Do you think bosoms will be in or out, this year?

25

JIMMY: Your teeth will be out in a minute, if you don't let go!
He makes a great effort to wrench himself free, but Cliff hangs on. They collapse to the floor C., below the table, struggling. Alison carries on with her ironing. This is routine, but she is getting close to breaking point, all the same. Cliff manages to break away, and finds himself in front of the ironing board. Jimmy springs up. They grapple.

ALISON: Look out, for heaven's sake! Oh, it's more like a zoo every day!
Jimmy makes a frantic, deliberate effort, and manages to push Cliff on to the ironing board, and into Alison. The board collapses. Cliff falls against her, and they end up in a heap on the floor. Alison cries out in pain. Jimmy looks down at them, dazed and breathless.

CLIFF: (*picking himself up*). She's hurt. Are you all right?

ALISON: Well, does it look like it!

CLIFF: She's burnt her arm on the iron.

JIMMY: Darling, I'm sorry.

ALISON: Get out!

JIMMY: I'm sorry, believe me. You think I did it on pur——

ALISON: (*her head shaking helplessly*). Clear out of my *sight*!
He stares at her uncertainly. Cliff nods to him, and he turns and goes out of the door.

CLIFF: Come and sit down.
He leads her to the armchair. R.
You look a bit white. Are you all right?

ALISON: Yes. I'm all right now.

CLIFF: Let's have a look at your arm. (*Examines it.*) Yes, it's quite red. That's going to be painful. What should I do with it?

ALISON: Oh, it's nothing much. A bit of soap on it will do. I never can remember what you do with burns.

CLIFF: I'll just pop down to the bathroom and get some. Are you sure you're all right?

ALISON: Yes.

CLIFF: (*crossing to door*). Won't be a minute.
EXIT.

She leans back in the chair, and looks up at the ceiling.
She breathes in deeply, and brings her hands up to her
face. She winces as she feels the pain in her arm, and she
lets it fall. She runs her hand through her hair.

ALISON: (*in a clenched whisper*). Oh, God!
Cliff re-enters with a bar of soap.

CLIFF: It's this scented muck. Do you think it'll be all right?

ALISON: That'll do.

CLIFF: Here we are then. Let's have your arm.
He kneels down beside her, and she holds out her arm.
I've put it under the tap. It's quite soft. I'll do it ever
so gently.
Very carefully, he rubs the soap over the burn.
All right? (*She nods.*) You're a brave girl.

ALISON: I don't feel very brave. (*Tears harshening her voice.*) I
really don't, Cliff. I don't think I can take much more.
(*Turns her head away.*) I think I feel rather sick.

CLIFF: All over now. (*Puts the soap down.*) Would you like me
to get you something?
*She shakes her head. He sits on the arm of the chair, and
puts his arm round her. She leans her head back on to him.*
Don't upset yourself, lovely.
*He massages the back of her neck, and she lets her head
fall forward.*

ALISON: Where is he?

CLIFF: In my room.

ALISON: What's he doing?

CLIFF: Lying on the bed. Reading, I think. (*Stroking her
neck*). That better?
She leans back, and closes her eyes again.

ALISON: Bless you.
He kisses the top of her head.

CLIFF: I don't think I'd have the courage to live on my own
again—in spite of everything. I'm pretty rough, and
pretty ordinary really, and I'd seem worse on my own.
And you get fond of people too, worse luck.

ALISON: I don't think I want anything more to do with love.
Any more. I can't take it on.

27

CLIFF: You're too young to start giving up. Too young, and too lovely. Perhaps I'd better put a bandage on that—do you think so?

ALISON: There's some on my dressing table.

Cliff crosses to the dressing table R.

I keep looking back, as far as I remember, and I can't think what it was to feel young, really young. Jimmy said the same thing to me the other day. I pretended not to be listening—because I knew that would hurt him, I suppose. And—of course—he got savage, like tonight. But I knew just what he meant. I suppose it would have been so easy to say "Yes, darling, I know just what you mean. I know what you're feeling." (*Shrugs.*) It's those easy things that seem to be so impossible with us.

Cliff stands down R., holding the bandage, his back to her.

CLIFF: I'm wondering how much longer I can go on watching you two tearing the insides out of each other. It looks pretty ugly sometimes.

ALISON: You wouldn't seriously think of leaving us, would you?

CLIFF: I suppose not. (*Crosses to her.*)

ALISON: I think I'm frightened. If only I knew what was going to happen.

CLIFF: (*kneeling on the arm of her chair*). Give it here. (*She holds out her arm.*) Yell out if I hurt you. (*He bandages it for her.*)

ALISON: (*staring at her outstretched arm*). Cliff——

CLIFF: Um? (*Slight pause.*) What is it, lovely?

ALISON: Nothing.

CLIFF: I said: what is it?

ALISON: You see——(*Hesitates.*) I'm pregnant.

CLIFF: (*after a few moments*). I'll need some scissors.

ALISON: They're over there.

CLIFF: (*crossing to the dressing table*). That is something, isn't it? When did you find this out?

ALISON: Few days ago. It was a bit of a shock.

CLIFF: Yes, I dare say.

28

ALISON: After three years of married life, I have to get caught out now.

CLIFF: None of us infallible, I suppose. (*Crosses to her.*) Must say I'm surprised though.

ALISON: It's always been out of the question. What with— this place, and no money, and oh—everything. He's resented it, I know. What can you do?

CLIFF: You haven't told him yet.

ALISON: Not yet.

CLIFF: What are you going to do?

ALISON: I've no idea.

CLIFF: (*having cut her bandage, he starts tying it*). That too tight?

ALISON: Fine, thank you.
She rises, goes to the ironing board, folds it up, and leans it against the food cupboard R.

CLIFF: Is it . . . Is it . . . ?

ALISON: Too late to avert the situation? (*Places the iron on the rack of the stove.*) I'm not certain yet. Maybe not. If not, there won't be any problem, will there?

CLIFF: And if it is too late?
Her face is turned away from him. She simply shakes her head.
Why don't you tell him now?
She kneels down to pick up the clothes on the floor, and folds them up.
After all, he does love you. You don't need me to tell you that.

ALISON: Can't you see? He'll suspect my motives at once. He never stops telling himself that I know how vulnerable he is. Tonight it might be all right—we'd make love. But later, we'd both lie awake, watching for the light to come through that little window, and dreading it. In the morning, he'd feel hoaxed, as if I were trying to kill him in the worst way of all. He'd watch me growing bigger every day, and I wouldn't dare to look at him.

CLIFF: You may have to face it, lovely.

29

ALISON: Jimmy's got his own private morality, as you know. What my mother calls "loose". It is pretty free, of course, but it's very harsh too. You know, it's funny, but we never slept together before we were married.

CLIFF: It certainly is—knowing him!

ALISON: We knew each other such a short time, everything moved at such a pace, we didn't have much opportunity. And, afterwards, he actually taunted me with my virginity. He was quite angry about it, as if I had deceived him in some strange way. He seemed to think an untouched woman would defile him.

CLIFF: I've never heard you talking like this about him. He'd be quite pleased.

ALISON: Yes, he would.

She gets up, the clothes folded over her arm.

Do you think he's right?

CLIFF: What about?

ALISON: Oh—everything.

CLIFF: Well, I suppose he and I think the same about a lot of things, because we're alike in some ways. We both come from working people, if you like. Oh I know some of his mother's relatives are pretty posh, but he hates them as much as he hates yours. Don't quite know why. Anyway, he gets on with me because I'm common. (*Grins.*) Common as dirt, that's me.

She puts her hand on his head, and strokes it thoughtfully.

ALISON: You think I should tell him about the baby?

He gets up, and puts his arm round her.

CLIFF: It'll be all right—you see. Tell him.

He kisses her. Enter Jimmy. He looks at them curiously, but without surprise. They are both aware of him, but make no sign of it. He crosses to the armchair L., and sits down next to them. He picks up a paper, and starts looking at it. Cliff glances at him, Alison's head against his cheek.

There you are, you old devil, you! Where have you been?

JIMMY: You know damn well where I've been. (*Without looking at her.*) How's your arm?

ALISON: Oh, it's all right. It wasn't much.

CLIFF: She's beautiful, isn't she?

JIMMY: You seem to think so.

Cliff and Alison still have their arms round one another.

CLIFF: Why the hell she married you, I'll never know.

JIMMY: You think she'd have been better off with you?

CLIFF: I'm not her type. Am I, dullin' ?

ALISON: I'm not sure what my type is.

JIMMY: Why don't you both get into bed, and have done with it.

ALISON: You know, I think he really means that.

JIMMY: I do. I can't concentrate with you two standing there like that.

CLIFF: He's just an old Puritan at heart.

JIMMY: Perhaps I am, at that. Anyway, you both look pretty silly slobbering over each other.

CLIFF: I think she's beautiful. And so do you, only you're too much of a pig to say so.

JIMMY: You're just a sexy little Welshman, and you know it! Mummy and Daddy turn pale, and face the east every time they remember she's married to me. But if they saw all this going on, they'd collapse. Wonder what they would do, incidentally. Send for the police I expect. (*Genuinely friendly.*) Have you got a cigarette?

ALISON: (*disengaging*). I'll have a look.

She goes to her handbag on the table C.

JIMMY: (*pointing at Cliff*). He gets more like a little mouse every day, doesn't he?

He is trying to re-establish himself.

He really does look like one. Look at those ears, and that face, and the little short legs.

ALISON: (*looking through her bag*). That's because he *is* a mouse.

CLIFF: Eek! Eek! I'm a mouse.

JIMMY: A randy little mouse.

CLIFF: (*dancing round the table, and squeaking*). I'm a mouse, I'm a mouse, I'm a randy little mouse. That's a mourris dance.

JIMMY: A what?

CLIFF: A *Mourris Dance*. That's a Morris Dance strictly for mice.

JIMMY: You stink. You really do. Do you know that?

CLIFF: Not as bad as you, you horrible old bear. (*Goes over to him, and grabs his foot.*) You're a stinking old bear, you hear me?

JIMMY: Let go of my foot, you whimsy little half-wit. You're making my stomach heave. I'm resting! If you don't let go, I'll cut off your nasty, great, slimy tail!
Cliff gives him a tug, and Jimmy falls to the floor. Alison watches them, relieved and suddenly full of affection.

ALISON: I've run out of cigarettes.
Cliff is dragging Jimmy along the floor by his feet.

JIMMY: (*yelling*). Go out and get me some cigarettes, and stop playing the fool!

CLIFF: O.K.
He lets go of Jimmy's legs suddenly, who yells again as his head bangs on the floor.

ALISON: Here's half a crown. (*Giving it h·m.*) The shop on the corner will be open.

CLIFF: Right you are. (*Kisses her on the forehead quickly.*) Don't forget. (*Crosses upstage to door.*)

JIMMY: Now get to hell out of here!

CLIFF: (*at door*). Hey, shorty!

JIMMY: What do you want?

CLIFF: Make a nice pot of tea.

JIMMY: (*getting up*). I'll kill you first.

CLIFF: (*grinning*). That's my boy!
EXIT.
Jimmy is now beside Alison, who is still looking through her handbag. She becomes aware of his nearness, and, after a few moments, closes it. He takes hold of her bandaged arm.

JIMMY: How's it feeling?

ALISON: Fine. It wasn't anything.

JIMMY: All this fooling about can get a bit dangerous.

32

He sits on the edge of the table, holding her hand.
I'm sorry.

ALISON: I know.

JIMMY: I mean it.

ALISON: There's no need.

JIMMY: I did it on purpose.

ALISON: Yes.

JIMMY: There's hardly a moment when I'm not—watching and wanting you. I've got to hit out somehow. Nearly four years of being in the same room with you, night and day, and I still can't stop my sweat breaking out when I see you doing—something as ordinary as leaning over an ironing board.
She strokes his head, not sure of herself yet.
(*sighing*). Trouble is—Trouble is you get used to people. Even their trivialities become indispensable to you. Indispensable, and a little mysterious.
He slides his head forward, against her, trying to catch his thoughts.
I think . . . I must have a lot of—old stock. . . . Nobody wants it. . . .
He puts his face against her belly. She goes on stroking his head, still on guard a little. Then he lifts his head, and they kiss passionately.
What are we going to do tonight?

ALISON: What would you like to do? Drink?

JIMMY: I know what I want now.
She takes his head in her hands and kisses him.

ALISON: Well, you'll have to wait till the proper time.

JIMMY: There's no such thing.

ALISON: Cliff will be back in a minute.

JIMMY: What did he mean by "don't forget"?

ALISON: Something I've been meaning to tell you.

JIMMY: (*kissing her again*). You're fond of him, aren't you?

ALISON: Yes, I am.

JIMMY: He's the only friend I seem to have left now. People go away. You never see them again. I can remember

33

lots of names—men and women. When I was at school
—Watson, Roberts, Davies. Jenny, Madeline, Hugh. . .
(*Pause.*) And there's Hugh's mum, of course. I'd
almost forgotten her. She's been a good friend to us,
if you like. She's even letting me buy the sweet-stall
off her in my own time. She only bought it for us,
anyway. She's so fond of you. I can never understand
why you're so—distant with her.

ALISON: (*alarmed at this threat of a different mood*). Jimmy—
please no!

JIMMY: (*staring at her anxious face*). You're very beautiful. A
beautiful, great-eyed squirrel.
She nods brightly, relieved.
Hoarding, nut-munching squirrel. (*She mimes this
delightedly.*) With highly polished, gleaming fur, and
an ostrich feather of a tail.

ALISON: Wheeeeeeeeee!

JIMMY: How I envy you.
He stands, her arms around his neck.

ALISON: Well, you're a jolly super bear, too. A really
sooooooooooooooooper, marvellous bear.

JIMMY: Bears and squirrels *are* marvellous.

ALISON: Marvellous *and* beautiful.
*She jumps up and down excitedly, making little "paw
gestures".*
Oooooooooh! Oooooooooh!

JIMMY: What the hell's that?

ALISON: That's a dance squirrels do when they're happy.
They embrace again.

JIMMY: What makes you think you're happy?

ALISON: Everything just seems all right suddenly. That's all.
Jimmy——

JIMMY: Yes?

ALISON: You know I told you I'd something to tell you?

JIMMY: Well?
Cliff appears in the doorway.

CLIFF: Didn't get any further than the front door. Miss
Drury hadn't gone to church after all. I couldn't get

34

away from her. (*To Alison.*) Someone on the phone for you.

ALISON: On the phone? Who on earth is it?

CLIFF: Helena something.

Jimmy and Alison look at each other quickly.

JIMMY: (*to Cliff*). Helena Charles?

CLIFF: That's it.

ALISON: Thank you, Cliff. (*Moves upstage.*) I won't be a minute.

CLIFF: You will. Old Miss Drury will keep you down there forever. She doesn't think we keep this place clean enough. (*Comes and sits in the armchair down R.*) Thought you were going to make me some tea, you rotter.

Jimmy makes no reply.

What's the matter, boyo?

JIMMY: (*slowly*). That bitch.

CLIFF: Who?

JIMMY: (*to himself*). Helena Charles.

CLIFF: Who is this Helena?

JIMMY: One of her old friends. And one of my natural enemies. You're sitting on my chair.

CLIFF: Where are we going for a drink?

JIMMY: I don't know.

CLIFF: Well, you were all for it earlier on.

JIMMY: What does she want? What would make her ring up? It can't be for anything pleasant. Oh well, we shall soon know. (*He settles on the table.*) Few minutes ago things didn't seem so bad either. I've just about had enough of this "expense of spirit" lark, as far as women are concerned. Honestly, it's enough to make you become a scoutmaster or something isn't it? Sometimes I almost envy old Gide and the Greek Chorus boys. Oh, I'm not saying that it mustn't be hell for them a lot of the time. But, at least, they do seem to have a cause—not a particularly good one, it's true. But plenty of them do seem to have a revolutionary fire about them, which is more than you can say for the rest of us.

35

Like Webster, for instance. He doesn't like me—they
hardly ever do.

*He is talking for the sake of it, only half listening to what
he is saying.*

I dare say he suspects me because I refuse to treat him
either as a clown or as a tragic hero. He's like a man
with a strawberry mark—he keeps thrusting it in your
face because he can't believe it doesn't interest or
horrify you particularly. (*Picks up Alison's handbag
thoughtfully, and starts looking through it.*) As if I give a
damn which way he likes his meat served up. I've got
my own strawberry mark—only it's in a different place.
No, as far as the Michaelangelo Brigade's concerned, I
must be a sort of right-wing deviationist. If the
Revolution ever comes, I'll be the first to be put up
against the wall, with all the other poor old liberals.

CLIFF: (*indicating Alison's handbag*). Wouldn't you say that
that was her private property?

JIMMY: You're quite right. But do you know something?
Living night and day with another human being has
made me predatory and suspicious. I know that the
only way of finding out exactly what's going on is to
catch them when they don't know you're looking.
When she goes out, I go through everything—trunks,
cases, drawers, bookcase, everything. Why? To see if
there is something of me somewhere, a reference to me.
I want to know if I'm being betrayed.

CLIFF: You look for trouble, don't you?

JIMMY: Only because I'm pretty certain of finding it. (*Brings
out a letter from the handbag.*) Look at that! Oh, I'm
such a fool. This is happening every five minutes of the
day. She gets letters. (*He holds it up.*) Letters from her
mother, letters in which I'm not mentioned at all
because my name is a dirty word. And what does she
do?

Enter Alison. He turns to look at her.

She writes long letters back to Mummy, and never

36

mentions me at all, because I'm just a dirty word to
her too.

He throws the letter down at her feet.

Well, what did your friend want?

ALISON: She's at the station. She's—coming over.

JIMMY: I see. She said "Can I come over?" And you said "My
husband, Jimmy—if you'll forgive me using such a
dirty word, will be delighted to see you. He'll kick your
face in!"

*He stands up, unable to sustain his anger, poised on the
table.*

ALISON: (*quietly*). She's playing with the company at the
Hippodrome this week, and she's got no digs. She can't
find anywhere to stay——

JIMMY: That I don't believe!

ALISON: So I said she could come here until she fixes something
else. Miss Drury's got a spare room downstairs.

JIMMY: Why not have her in here? Did you tell her to bring
her armour? Because she's going to need it!

ALISON: (*vehemently*). Oh why don't you shut up, please!

JIMMY: Oh, my dear wife, you've got so much to learn. I only
hope you learn it one day. If only something—
something would happen to you, and wake you out of
your beauty sleep! (*Coming in close to her.*) If you could
have a child, and it would die. Let it grow, let a
recognisable human face emerge from that little mass of
indiarubber and wrinkles. (*She retreats away from him.*)
Please—if only I could watch you face that. I wonder if
you might even become a recognisable human being
yourself. But I doubt it.

*She moves away, stunned, and leans on the gas stove down
L. He stands rather helplessly on his own.*

Do you know I have never known the great pleasure of
lovemaking when I didn't desire it myself. Oh, it's not
that she hasn't her own kind of passion. She has the
passion of a python. She just devours me whole every
time, as if I were some over-large rabbit.

That's me. That bulge around her navel—if you're

37

wondering what it is—it's me. Me, buried alive down there, and going mad, smothered in that peaceful looking coil. Not a sound, not a flicker from her—she doesn't even rumble a little. You'd think that this indigestible mess would stir up some kind of tremor in those distended, overfed tripes—but not her!

Crosses up to the door.

She'll go on sleeping and devouring until there's nothing left of me.

EXIT.

Alison's head goes back as if she were about to make some sound. But her mouth remains open and trembling, as Cliff looks on.

CURTAIN

END OF ACT I

ACT II

SCENE I

Two weeks later. Evening.
ALISON is standing over the gas stove, pouring water
from the kettle into a large teapot. She is only wearing
a slip, and her feet are bare. In the room across the hall,
JIMMY is playing on his jazz trumpet, in intermittent
bursts. ALISON takes the pot to the table C., which is
laid for four people. The Sunday paper jungle around
the two armchairs is as luxuriant as ever. It is late
afternoon, the end of a hot day. She wipes her forehead.
She crosses to the dressing table R., takes out a pair of
stockings from one of the drawers, and sits down on the
small chair beside it to put them on. While she is doing
this, the door opens and HELENA enters. She is the same
age as ALISON, medium height, carefully and
expensively dressed. Now and again, when she allows
her rather judicial expression of alertness to soften, she
is very attractive. Her sense of matriarchal authority
makes most men who meet her anxious, not only to
please but impress, as if she were the gracious
representative of visiting royalty. In this case, the
royalty of that middle-class womanhood, which is so
eminently secure in its divine rights, that it can afford
to tolerate the parliament, and reasonably free
assembly of its menfolk. Even from other young
women, like ALISON, she receives her due of respect and
admiration. In JIMMY, as one would expect, she arouses
all the rabble-rousing instincts of his spirit. And she is
not accustomed to having to defend herself against
catcalls. However, her sense of modestly exalted
responsibility enables her to behave with an impressive

39

show of strength and dignity, although the strain of this is beginning to tell on her a little. She is carrying a large salad colander.

ALISON: Did you manage all right?

HELENA: Of course. I've prepared most of the meals in the last week, you know.

ALISON: Yes, you have. It's been wonderful having someone to help. Another woman, I mean.

HELENA: (*crossing down L.*). I'm enjoying it. Although I don't think I shall ever get used to having to go down to the bathroom every time I want some water for something.

ALISON: It is primitive, isn't it?

HELENA: Yes. It is rather.

She starts tearing up green salad on to four plates, which she takes from the food cupboard.

Looking after one man is really enough, but two is rather an undertaking.

ALISON: Oh, Cliff looks after himself, more or less. In fact, he helps me quite a lot.

HELENA: Can't say I'd noticed it.

ALISON: You've been doing it instead, I suppose.

HELENA: I see.

ALISON: You've settled in so easily somehow.

HELENA: Why shouldn't I?

ALISON: It's not exactly what you're used to, is it?

HELENA: And are you used to it?

ALISON: Everything seems very different here now—with you here.

HELENA: Does it?

ALISON: Yes. I was on my own before——

HELENA: Now you've got me. So you're not sorry you asked me to stay?

ALISON: Of course not. Did you tell him his tea was ready?

HELENA: I banged on the door of Cliff's room, and yelled. He didn't answer, but he must have heard. I don't know where Cliff is.

ALISON: (*leaning back in her chair*). I thought I'd feel cooler after

40

a bath, but I feel hot again already. God, I wish he'd lose that damned trumpet.

HELENA: I imagine that's for my benefit.

ALISON: Miss Drury will ask us to go soon, I know it. Thank goodness she isn't in. Listen to him.

HELENA: Does he drink?

ALISON: Drink? (*Rather startled.*) He's not an alcoholic, if that's what you mean.

They both pause, listening to the trumpet.

He'll have the rest of the street banging on the door next.

HELENA: (*pondering*). It's almost as if he wanted to kill someone with it. And me in particular. I've never seen such hatred in someone's eyes before. It's slightly horrifying. Horrifying (*crossing to food cupboard for tomatoes, beetroot and cucumber*) and oddly exciting.

Alison faces her dressing mirror, and brushes her hair.

ALISON: He had his own jazz band once. That was when he was still a student, before I knew him. I rather think he'd like to start another, and give up the stall altogether.

HELENA: Is Cliff in love with you?

ALISON: (*stops brushing for a moment*). No . . . I don't think so.

HELENA: And what about you? You look as though I've asked you a rather peculiar question. The way things are, you might as well be frank with me. I only want to help. After all, your behaviour together is a little strange—by most people's standards, to say the least.

ALISON: You mean you've seen us embracing each other?

HELENA: Well, it doesn't seem to go on as much as it did, I admit. Perhaps he finds my presence inhibiting—even if Jimmy's isn't.

ALISON: We're simply fond of each other—there's no more to it than that.

HELENA: Darling, really! It can't be as simple as that.

ALISON: You mean there must be something physical too? I suppose there is, but it's not exactly a consuming passion with either of us. It's just a relaxed, cheerful sort of thing, like being warm in bed. You're too comfortable to bother about moving for the sake of some other pleasure.

HELENA: I find it difficult to believe anyone's that lazy!

ALISON: I think *we* are.

HELENA: And what about Jimmy? After all, he is your husband. Do you mean to say he actually approves of it?

ALISON: It isn't easy to explain. It's what he would call a question of allegiances, and he expects you to be pretty literal about them. Not only about himself and all the things he believes in, his present and his future, but his past as well. All the people he admires and loves, and has loved. The friends he used to know, people I've never even known—and probably wouldn't have liked. His father, who died years ago. Even the other women he's loved. Do you understand?

HELENA: Do you?

ALISON: I've tried to. But I still can't bring myself to feel the way he does about things. I can't believe that he's right somehow.

HELENA: Well, that's something, anyway.

ALISON: If things have worked out with Cliff, it's because he's kind and lovable, and I've grown genuinely fond of him. But it's been a fluke. It's worked because Cliff is such a nice person anyway. With Hugh, it was quite different.

HELENA: Hugh?

ALISON: Hugh Tanner. He and Jimmy were friends almost from childhood. Mrs. Tanner is his mother——

HELENA: Oh yes—the one who started him off in the sweet business.

ALISON: That's right. Well, after Jimmy and I were married, we'd no money—about eight pounds ten in actual fact —and no home. He didn't even have a job. He'd only left the university about a year. (*Smiles.*) No—left. I don't think one "comes down" from Jimmy's university. According to him, it's not even red brick, but white tile. Anyway, we went off to live in Hugh's flat. It was over a warehouse in Poplar.

42

HELENA: Yes. I remember seeing the postmark on your letters.

ALISON: Well, that was where I found myself on my wedding night. Hugh and I disliked each other on sight, and Jimmy knew it. He was so proud of us both, so pathetically anxious that we should take to each other. Like a child showing off his toys. We had a little wedding celebration, and the three of us tried to get tight on some cheap port they'd brought in. Hugh got more and more subtly insulting—he'd a rare talent for that. Jimmy got steadily depressed, and I just sat there, listening to their talk, looking and feeling very stupid. For the first time in my life, I was cut off from the kind of people I'd always known, my family, my friends, everybody. And I'd burnt my boats. After all those weeks of brawling with Mummy and Daddy about Jimmy, I knew I couldn't appeal to them without looking foolish and cheap. It was just before the General Election, I remember, and Nigel was busy getting himself into Parliament. He didn't have time for anyone but his constituents. Oh, he'd have been sweet and kind, I know.

HELENA: (moving in C.). Darling, why didn't you come to me?

ALISON: You were away on tour in some play, I think.

HELENA: So I was.

ALISON: Those next few months at the flat in Poplar were a nightmare. I suppose I must be soft and squeamish, and snobbish, but I felt as though I'd been dropped in a jungle. I couldn't believe that two people, two educated people could be so savage, and so—so uncompromising. Mummy has always said that Jimmy is utterly ruthless, but she hasn't met Hugh. He takes the first prize for ruthlessness—from all comers. Together, they were frightening. They both came to regard me as a sort of hostage from those sections of society they had declared war on.

HELENA: How were you living all this time?

ALISON: I had a tiny bit coming in from a few shares I had left, but it hardly kept us. Mummy had made me sign everything else over to her, in trust, when she knew I was really going to marry Jimmy.

HELENA: Just as well, I imagine.

ALISON: They soon thought of a way out of that. A brilliant campaign. They started inviting themselves—through me—to people's houses, friends of Nigel's and mine, friends of Daddy's, oh everyone: The Arksdens, the Tarnatts, the Wains——

HELENA: Not the Wains?

ALISON: Just about everyone I'd ever known. Your people must have been among the few we missed out. It was just enemy territory to them, and, as I say, they used me as a hostage. We'd set out from headquarters in Poplar, and carry out our raids on the enemy in W.1, S.W.1., S.W.3. and W.8. In my name, we'd gatecrash everywhere—cocktails, week-ends, even a couple of houseparties. I used to hope that one day, somebody would have the guts to slam the door in our faces, but they didn't. They were too well-bred, and probably sorry for me as well. Hugh and Jimmy despised them for it. So we went on plundering them, wolfing their food and drinks, and smoking their cigars like ruffians. Oh, they enjoyed themselves.

HELENA: Apparently.

ALISON: Hugh fairly revelled in the role of the barbarian invader. Sometimes I thought he might even dress the part—you know, furs, spiked helmet, sword. He even got a fiver out of old Man Wain once. Blackmail, of course. People would have signed almost anything to get rid of us. He told him that we were about to be turned out of our flat for not paying the rent. At least it was true.

HELENA: I don't understand you. You must have been crazy.

ALISON: Afraid more than anything.

HELENA: But letting them do it! Letting them get away with it! You managed to stop them stealing the silver, I suppose?

ALISON: Oh, they knew their guerrilla warfare better than that.

44

Hugh tried to seduce some fresh-faced young girl at the Arksdens' once, but that was the only time we were more or less turned out.

HELENA: It's almost unbelievable. I don't understand your part in it all. Why? That's what I don't see. Why did you——

ALISON: Marry him? There must be about six different answers. When the family came back from India, everything seemed, I don't know—unsettled? Anyway, Daddy seemed remote and rather irritable. And Mummy—well, you know Mummy. I didn't have much to worry about. I didn't know I was born as Jimmy says. I met him at a party. I remember it so clearly. I was almost twenty-one. The men there all looked as though they distrusted him, and as for the women, they were all intent on showing their contempt for this rather odd creature, but no one seemed quite sure how to do it. He'd come to the party on a bicycle, he told me, and there was oil all over his dinner jacket. It had been such a lovely day, and he'd been in the sun. Everything about him seemed to burn, his face, the edges of his hair glistened and seemed to spring off his head, and his eyes were so blue and full of the sun. He looked so young and frail, in spite of the tired line of his mouth. I knew I was taking on more than I was ever likely to be capable of bearing, but there never seemed to be any choice. Well, the howl of outrage and astonishment went up from the family, and that did it. Whether or no he was in love with me, that did it. He made up his mind to marry me. They did just about everything they could think of to stop us.

HELENA: Yes, it wasn't a very pleasant business. But you can see their point.

ALISON: Jimmy went into battle with his axe swinging round his head—frail, and so full of fire. I had never seen anything like it. The old story of the knight in shining armour—except that his armour didn't really shine very much.

HELENA: And what about Hugh?

45

ALISON: Things got steadily worse between us. He and Jimmy even went to some of Nigel's political meetings. They took bunches of their Poplar cronies with them, and broke them up for him.

HELENA: He's really a savage, isn't he?

ALISON: Well, Hugh was writing some novel or other, and he made up his mind he must go abroad—to China, or some God-forsaken place. He said that England was finished for us, anyway. All the old gang was back— Dame Alison's Mob, as he used to call it. The only real hope was to get out, and try somewhere else. He wanted us to go with him, but Jimmy refused to go. There was a terrible, bitter row over it. Jimmy accused Hugh of giving up, and he thought it was wrong of him to go off forever, and leave his mother all on her own. He was upset by the whole idea. They quarrelled for days over it. I almost wished they'd both go, and leave me behind. Anyway, they broke up. A few months later we came up here, and Hugh went off to find the New Millennium on his own. Sometimes, I think Hugh's mother blames me for it all. Jimmy too, in a way, although he's never said so. He never mentions it. But whenever that woman looks at me, I can feel her thinking "If it hadn't been for you, everything would have been all right. We'd have all been happy." Not that I dislike her—I don't. She's very sweet, in fact. Jimmy seems to adore her principally because she's been poor almost all her life, and she's frankly ignorant. I'm quite aware how snobbish that sounds, but it happens to be the truth.

HELENA: Alison, listen to me. You've got to make up your mind what you're going to do. You're going to have a baby, and you have a new responsibility. Before, it was different—there was only yourself at stake. But you can't go on living in this way any longer. (*To her.*)

ALISON: I'm so tired. I dread him coming into the room.

HELENA: Why haven't you told him you're going to have a child?

ALISON: I don't know. (*Suddenly anticipating Helena's train of thought*.) Oh, it's his all right. There couldn't be any doubt of that. You see——(*she smiles*). I've never really wanted anyone else.

HELENA: Listen, darling—you've got to tell him. Either he learns to behave like anyone else, and looks after you——

ALISON: Or?

HELENA: Or you must get out of this mad-house. (*Trumpet crescendo*.) This menagerie. He doesn't seem to know what love or anything else means.

ALISON: (*pointing to chest of drawers up R.*). You see that bear, and that squirrel? Well, that's him, and that's me.

HELENA: Meaning?

ALISON: The game we play: bears and squirrels, squirrels and bears.

Helena looks rather blank.

Yes, it's quite mad, I know. Quite mad. (*Picks up the two animals*.) That's him. . . . And that's me. . . .

HELENA: I didn't realise he was a bit fey, as well as everything else!

ALISON: Oh, there's nothing fey about Jimmy. It's just all we seem to have left. Or had left. Even bears and squirrels seem to have gone their own ways now.

HELENA: Since I arrived?

ALISON: It started during those first months we had alone together—after Hugh went abroad. It was the one way of escaping from everything—a sort of unholy priest-hole of being animals to one another. We could become little furry creatures with little furry brains. Full of dumb, uncomplicated affection for each other. Playful, careless creatures in their own cosy zoo for two. A silly symphony for people who couldn't bear the pain of being human beings any longer. And now, even they are dead, poor little silly animals. They were all love, and no brains. (*Puts them back*.)

HELENA: (*gripping her arm*). Listen to me. You've got to fight him. Fight, or get out. Otherwise, he *will* kill you.

Enter Cliff.

CLIFF: There you are, dullin'. Hullo, Helena. Tea ready?

47

ALISON: Yes, dear, it's all ready. Give Jimmy a call, will you?

CLIFF: Right. (*Yelling back through door.*) Hey, you horrible man! Stop that bloody noise, and come and get your tea! (*Coming in C.*) Going out?

HELENA: (*crossing to L.*). Yes.

CLIFF: Pictures?

HELENA: No. (*Pause.*) Church.

CLIFF: (*really surprised*). Oh! I see. Both of you?

HELENA: Yes. Are you coming?

CLIFF: Well. . . . I—I haven't read the papers properly yet. Tea, tea, tea! Let's have some tea, shall we?

He sits at the upstage end of the table. Helena puts the four plates of salad on it, sits down L., and they begin the meal. Alison is making up her face at her dressing table. Presently, Jimmy enters. He places his trumpet on the bookcase, and comes above the table.

Hullo, boyo. Come and have your tea. That blinkin' trumpet—why don't you stuff it away somewhere?

JIMMY: You like it all right. Anyone who doesn't like real jazz, hasn't any feeling either for music or people.

He sits R. end of table.

HELENA: Rubbish.

JIMMY: (*to Cliff*). That seems to prove my point for you. Did you know that Webster played the banjo?

CLIFF: No, does he really?

HELENA: He said he'd bring it along next time he came.

ALISON: (*muttering*). Oh, no!

JIMMY: Why is it that nobody knows how to treat the papers in this place? Look at them. I haven't even glanced at them yet—not the posh ones, anyway.

CLIFF: By the way, can I look at your *New*——

JIMMY: No, you can't! (*Loudly.*) You want anything, you pay for it. Like I have to. Price——

CLIFF: Price ninepence, obtainable from any bookstall! You're a mean old man, that's what you are.

JIMMY: What do you want to read it for, anyway? You've no intellect, no curiosity. It all just washes over you. Am I right?

48

CLIFF: Right.

JIMMY: What are you, you Welsh trash?

CLIFF: Nothing, that's what I am.

JIMMY: Nothing are you? Blimey you ought to be Prime Minister. You must have been talking to some of my wife's friends. They're a very intellectual set, aren't they? I've seen 'em.

Cliff and Helena carry on with their meal.

They all sit around feeling very spiritual, with their mental hands on each other's knees, discussing sex as if it were the Art of Fugue. If you don't want to be an emotional old spinster, just you listen to your dad!

He starts eating. The silent hostility of the two women has set him off on the scent, and he looks quite cheerful, although the occasional, thick edge of his voice belies it.

You know your trouble, son? Too anxious to please.

HELENA: Thank heavens somebody is!

JIMMY: You'll end up like one of those chocolate meringues my wife is so fond of. My wife—that's the one on the tom-toms behind me. Sweet and sticky on the outside, and sink your teeth in it, (*savouring every word*) inside, all white, messy and disgusting. (*Offering teapot sweetly to Helena.*) Tea?

HELENA: Thank you.

He smiles, and pours out a cup for her.

JIMMY: That's how you'll end up, my boy—black hearted, evil minded and vicious.

HELENA: (*taking cup.*) Thank you.

JIMMY: And those old favourites, your friends and mine: sycophantic, phlegmatic, and, of course, top of the bill—pusillanimous.

HELENA: (*to Alison*). Aren't you going to have your tea?

ALISON: Won't be long.

JIMMY: Thought of the title for a new song today. It's called "You can quit hanging round my counter Mildred 'cos you'll find my position is closed". (*Turning to Alison suddenly.*) Good?

ALISON: Oh, very good.

JIMMY: Thought you'd like it. If I can slip in a religious angle, it should be a big hit. (*To Helena.*) Don't you think so? I was thinking you might help me there. (*She doesn't reply.*) It might help you if I recite the lyrics. Let's see now, it's something like this:

> I'm so tired of necking,
> of pecking, home wrecking,
> of empty bed blues—
> just pass me the booze.
> I'm tired of being hetero
> Rather ride on the metero
> Just pass me the booze.
> This perpetual whoring
> Gets quite dull and boring
> So avoid that old python coil
> And pass me the celibate oil.
> You can quit etc.

No?

CLIFF: Very good, boyo.

JIMMY: Oh, yes, and I know what I meant to tell you—I wrote a poem while I was at the market yesterday. If you're interested, which you obviously are. (*To Helena.*) It should appeal to you, in particular. It's soaked in the theology of Dante, with a good slosh of Eliot as well. It starts off "There are no dry cleaners in Cambodia!"

CLIFF: What do you call it?

JIMMY: "The Cess Pool". Myself being a stone dropped in it, you see——

CLIFF: You should be dropped in it, all right.

HELENA: (*to Jimmy*). Why do you try so hard to be unpleasant? *He turns very deliberately, delighted that she should rise to the bait so soon—he's scarcely in his stride yet.*

JIMMY: What's that?

HELENA: Do you have to be so offensive?

JIMMY: You mean now? You think I'm being offensive? You under-estimate me. (*Turning to Alison.*) Doesn't she?

HELENA: I think you're a very tiresome young man.

50

A slight pause as his delight catches up with him. He roars with laughter.

JIMMY: Oh dear, oh dear! My wife's friends! Pass Lady Bracknell the cucumber sandwiches, will you?
He returns to his meal, but his curiosity about Alison's preparations at the mirror won't be denied any longer. He turns round casually, and speaks to her.
Going out?

ALISON: That's right.

JIMMY: On a Sunday evening in this town? Where on earth are you going?

ALISON: (*rising*). I'm going out with Helena.

JIMMY: That's not a direction—that's an affliction.
She crosses to the table, and sits down C. He leans forward, and addresses her again.
I didn't ask you what was the matter with you. I asked you where you were going.

HELENA: (*steadily*). She's going to church.
He has been prepared for some plot, but he is as genuinely surprised by this as Cliff was a few minutes earlier.

JIMMY: You're doing what?
Silence.
Have you gone out of your mind or something? (*To Helena.*) You're determined to win her, aren't you? So it's come to this now! How feeble can you get? (*His rage mounting within.*) When I think of what I did, what I endured, to get you out——

ALISON: (*recognising an onslaught on the way, starts to panic*). Oh yes, we all know what you did for me! You rescued me from the wicked clutches of my family, and all my friends! I'd still be rotting away at home, if you hadn't ridden up on your charger, and carried me off!
The wild note in her voice has re-assured him. His anger cools and hardens. His voice is quite calm when he speaks.

JIMMY: The funny thing is, you know, I really did have to ride up on a white charger—off white, really. Mummy locked her up in their eight bedroomed castle, didn't she

51

There is no limit to what the middle-aged mummy will do in the holy crusade against ruffians like me. Mummy and I took one quick look at each other, and, from then on, the age of chivalry was dead. I knew that, to protect her innocent young, she wouldn't hesitate to cheat, lie, bully and blackmail. Threatened with me, a young man without money, background or even looks, she'd bellow like a rhinoceros in labour—enough to make every male rhino for miles turn white, and pledge himself to celibacy. But even I under-estimated her strength. Mummy may look over-fed and a bit flabby on the outside, but don't let that well-bred guzzler fool you. Underneath all that, she's armour plated——

He clutches wildly for something to shock Helena with.
She's as rough as a night in a Bombay brothel, and as tough as a matelot's arm. She's probably in that bloody cistern, taking down every word we say. (*Kicks cistern.*) Can you 'ear me, mother. (*Sits on it, beats like bongo drums.*) Just about get her in there. Let me give you an example of this lady's tactics. You may have noticed that I happen to wear my hair rather long. Now, if my wife is honest, or concerned enough to explain, she could tell you that this is not due to any dark, unnatural instincts I possess, but because (a) I can usually think of better things than a haircut to spend two bob on, and (b) I prefer long hair. But that obvious, innocent explanation didn't appeal to Mummy at all. So she hires detectives to watch me, to see if she can't somehow get me into the *News of the World.* All so that I shan't carry off her daughter on that poor old charger of mine, all tricked out and caparisoned in discredited passions and ideals! The old grey mare that actually once led the charge against the old order—well, she certainly ain't what she used to be. It was all she could do to carry me, but your weight (*to Alison*) was too much for her. She just dropped dead on the way.

CLIFF: (*quietly*). Don't let's brawl, boyo. It won't do any good.

JIMMY: Why *don't* we brawl? It's the only thing left I'm any good at.

CLIFF: Jimmy, boy——

JIMMY: (*to Alison*). You've let this genuflecting sin jobber win you over, haven't you? She's got you back, hasn't she?

HELENA: Oh for heaven's sake, don't be such a bully! You've no right to talk about her mother like that!

JIMMY: (*capable of anything now*). I've got every right. That old bitch should be dead! (*To Alison.*) Well? Aren't I right?
Cliff and Helena look at Alison tensely, but she just gazes at her plate.
I said she's an old bitch, and should be dead! What's the matter with you? Why don't you leap to her defence!
Cliff gets up quickly, and takes his arm.

CLIFF: Jimmy, don't!
Jimmy pushes him back savagely, and he sits down helplessly, turning his head away on to his hand.

JIMMY: If someone said something like that about me, she'd react soon enough—she'd spring into her well known lethargy, and say nothing! I say she ought to be dead. (*He brakes for a fresh spurt later. He's saving his strength for the knock-out.*) My God, those worms will need a good dose of salts the day they get through her! Oh what a bellyache you've got coming to you, my little wormy ones! Alison's mother is on the way! (*In what he intends to be a comic declamatory voice.*) She will pass away, my friends, leaving a trail of worms gasping for laxatives behind her—from purgatives to purgatory.
He smiles down at Alison, but still she hasn't broken. Cliff won't look at them. Only Helena looks at him. Denied the other two, he addresses her.
Is anything the matter?

HELENA: I feel rather sick, that's all. Sick with contempt and loathing.
He can feel her struggling on the end of his line, and he looks at her rather absently.

JIMMY: One day, when I'm no longer spending my days

running a sweet-stall, I may write a book about us all. It's all here. (*Slapping his forehead.*) Written in flames a mile high. And it won't be recollected in tranquillity either, picking daffodils with Auntie Wordsworth. It'll be recollected in fire, and blood. My blood.

HELENA: (*thinking patient reasonableness may be worth a try*). She simply said that she's going to church with me. I don't see why that calls for this incredible outburst.

JIMMY: Don't you? Perhaps you're not as clever as I thought.

HELENA: You think the world's treated you pretty badly, don't you?

ALISON: (*turning her face away L.*). Oh, don't try and take his suffering away from him—he'd be lost without it.
He looks at her in surprise, but he turns back to Helena. Alison can have her turn again later.

JIMMY: I thought this play you're touring in finished up on Saturday week?

HELENA: That's right.

JIMMY: Eight days ago, in fact.

HELENA: Alison wanted me to stay.

JIMMY: What are you plotting?

HELENA: Don't you think we've had enough of the heavy villain?

JIMMY: (*to Alison*). You don't believe in all that stuff. Why you don't believe in anything. You're just doing it to be vindictive, aren't you? Why—why are you letting her influence you like this?

ALISON: (*starting to break*). Why, why, why, why! (*Putting her hands over her ears.*) That word's pulling my head off!

JIMMY: And as long as you're around, I'll go on using it.
He crosses down to the armchair, and seats himself on the back of it. He addresses Helena's back.

JIMMY: The last time she was in a church was when she was married to me. I expect that surprises you, doesn't it? It was expediency, pure and simple. We were in a hurry, you see. (*The comedy of this strikes him at once, and he laughs.*) Yes, we were actually in a hurry! Lusting for the slaughter! Well, the local registrar was a particular pal of Daddy's, and we knew he'd spill the

54

beans to the Colonel like a shot. So we had to seek out
some local vicar who didn't know him quite so well.
But it was no use. When my best man—a chap I'd met
in the pub that morning—and I turned up, Mummy
and Daddy were in the church already. They'd found
out at the last moment, and had come to watch the
execution carried out. How I remember looking down
at them, full of beer for breakfast, and feeling a bit
buzzed. Mummy was slumped over her pew in a heap
—the noble, female rhino, pole-axed at last! And Daddy
sat beside her, upright and unafraid, dreaming of his
days among the Indian Princes, and unable to believe
he'd left his horsewhip at home. Just the two of them
in that empty church—them and me. (*Coming out of
his remembrance suddenly.*) I'm not sure what happened
after that. We must have been married, I suppose. I
think I remember being sick in the vestry. (*To Alison.*)
Was I?

HELENA: Haven't you finished?
*He can smell blood again, and he goes on calmly,
cheerfully.*

JIMMY: (*to Alison*). Are you going to let yourself be taken in by
this saint in Dior's clothing? I will tell you the simple
truth about her. (*Articulating with care.*) She is a cow.
I wouldn't mind that so much, but she seems to have
become a sacred cow as well!

CLIFF: You've gone too far, Jimmy. Now dry up!

HELENA: Oh, let him go on.

JIMMY: (*to Cliff*). I suppose you're going over to that side as
well. Well, why don't you? Helena will help to make it
pay off for you. She's an expert in the New Economics
—the Economics of the Supernatural. It's all a simple
matter of payments and penalties. (*Rises.*) She's one of
those apocalyptic share pushers who are spreading all
those rumours about a transfer of power.
His imagination is racing, and the words pour out.
Reason and Progress, the old firm, is selling out!
Everyone get out while the going's good. Those

55

forgotten shares you had in the old traditions, the old beliefs are going up—up and up and up. (*Moves up L.*) There's going to be a change over. A new Board of Directors, who are going to see that the dividends are always attractive, and that they go to the right people. (*Facing them.*) Sell out everything you've got: all those stocks in the old, free inquiry. (*Crosses to above table.*) The Big Crash is coming, you can't escape it, so get in on the ground floor with Helena and her friends while there's still time. And there isn't much of it left. Tell me, what could be more gilt-edged than the next world! It's a capital gain, and it's all yours.

He moves round the table, back to his chair R.

You see, I know Helena and her kind so very well. In fact, her kind are everywhere, you can't move for them. They're a romantic lot. They spend their time mostly looking forward to the past. The only place they can see the light is the Dark Ages. She's moved long ago into a lovely little cottage of the soul, cut right off from the ugly problems of the twentieth century altogether. She prefers to be cut off from all the conveniences we've fought to get for centuries. She'd rather go down to the ecstatic little shed at the bottom of the garden to relieve her sense of guilt. Our Helena is full of ecstatic wind— (*he leans across the table at her*) aren't you?

He waits for her to reply.

HELENA: (*quite calmly*). It's a pity you've been so far away all this time. I would probably have slapped your face.

They look into each other's eyes across the table. He moves slowly up, above Cliff, until he is beside her.

You've behaved like this ever since I first came.

JIMMY: Helena, have you ever watched somebody die?

She makes a move to rise.

No, don't move away.

She remains seated, and looks up at him.

It doesn't look dignified enough for you.

HELENA: (*like ice*). If you come any nearer, I will slap your face.

He looks down at her, a grin smouldering round his mouth.

56

JIMMY: I hope you won't make the mistake of thinking for one moment that I am a gentleman.

HELENA: I'm not very likely to do that.

JIMMY: (*bringing his face close to hers*). I've no public school scruples about hitting girls. (*Gently.*) If you slap my face—by God, I'll lay you out!

HELENA: You probably would. You're the type.

JIMMY: You bet I'm the type. I'm the type that detests physical violence. Which is why, if I find some woman trying to cash in on what she thinks is my defenceless chivalry by lashing out with her frail little fists, I lash back at her.

HELENA: Is that meant to be subtle, or just plain Irish?

His grin widens.

JIMMY: I think you and I understand one another all right. But you haven't answered my question. I said: have you watched somebody die?

HELENA: No, I haven't.

JIMMY: Anyone who's never watched somebody die is suffering from a pretty bad case of virginity.

His good humour of a moment ago deserts him, as he begins to remember.

For twelve months, I watched my father dying—when I was ten years old. He'd come back from the war in Spain, you see. And certain god-fearing gentlemen there had made such a mess of him, he didn't have long left to live. Everyone knew it—even I knew it.

He moves R.

But, you see, I was the only one who cared. (*Turns to the window.*) His family were embarrassed by the whole business. Embarrassed and irritated. (*Looking out.*) As for my mother, all she could think about was the fact that she had allied herself to a man who seemed to be on the wrong side in all things. My mother was all for being associated with minorities, provided they were the smart, fashionable ones.

He moves up C. again.

We all of us waited for him to die. The family sent

57

him a cheque every month, and hoped he'd get on with it quietly, without too much vulgar fuss. My mother looked after him without complaining, and that was about all. Perhaps she pitied him. I suppose she was capable of that. (*With a kind of appeal in his voice.*) But *I* was the only one who cared!

He moves L., behind the armchair.

Every time I sat on the edge of his bed, to listen to him talking or reading to me, I had to fight back my tears. At the end of twelve months, I was a veteran.

He leans forward on the back of the armchair.

All that that feverish failure of a man had to listen to him was a small, frightened boy. I spent hour upon hour in that tiny bedroom. He would talk to me for hours, pouring out all that was left of his life to one, lonely, bewildered little boy, who could barely understand half of what he said. All he could feel was the despair and the bitterness, the sweet, sickly smell of a dying man.

He moves around the chair.

You see, I learnt at an early age what it was to be angry—angry and helpless. And I can never forget it. (*Sits.*) I knew more about—love . . . betrayal . . . and death, when I was ten years old than you will probably ever know all your life.

They all sit silently. Presently, Helena rises.

HELENA: Time we went.

Alison nods.

I'll just get my things together. (*Crosses to door.*) I'll see you downstairs.

EXIT.

A slight pause.

JIMMY: (*not looking at her, almost whispering*). Doesn't it matter to you—what people do to me? What are you trying to do to me? I've given you just everything. Doesn't it mean *anything* to you?

Her back stiffens. His axe-swinging bravado has vanished, and his voice crumples in disabled rage.

58

JIMMY: You Judas! You phlegm! She's taking you with her, and you're so bloody feeble, you'll let her do it!

Alison suddenly takes hold of her cup, and hurls it on the floor. He's drawn blood at last. She looks down at the pieces on the floor, and then at him. Then she crosses, R., takes out a dress on a hanger, and slips it on. As she is zipping up the side, she feels giddy, and she has to lean against the wardrobe for support. She closes her eyes.

ALISON: *(softly)*. All I want is a little peace.

JIMMY: Peace! God! She wants peace! *(Hardly able to get his words out.)* My heart is so full, I feel ill—and she wants peace!

She crosses to the bed to put on her shoes. Cliff gets up from the table, and sits in the armchair R. He picks up a paper, and looks at that. Jimmy has recovered slightly, and manages to sound almost detached.

I rage, and shout my head off, and everyone thinks "poor chap!" or "what an objectionable young man!" But that girl there can twist your arm off with her silence. I've sat in this chair in the dark for hours. And, although she knows I'm feeling as I feel now, she's turned over, and gone to sleep. *(He gets up and faces Cliff, who doesn't look up from his paper.)* One of us is crazy. One of us is mean and stupid and crazy. Which is it? Is it me? Is it me, standing here like an hysterical girl, hardly able to get my words out? Or is it her? Sitting there, putting on her shoes to go out with that—— *(But inspiration has deserted him by now.)* Which is it?

Cliff is still looking down at his paper.

I wish to heaven you'd try loving her, that's all.

He moves up C., watching her look for her gloves.

Perhaps, one day, you may want to come back. I shall wait for that day. I want to stand up in your tears, and splash about in them, and sing. I want to be there when you grovel. I want to be there, I want to watch it, I want the front seat.

Helena enters, carrying two prayer books.

I want to see your face rubbed in the mud—that's all
I can hope for. There's nothing else I want any longer.

HELENA: (*after a moment*). There's a 'phone call for you.

JIMMY: (*turning*). Well, it can't be anything good, can it?
HE GOES OUT.

HELENA: All ready?

ALISON: Yes—I think so.

HELENA: You feel all right, don't you? (*She nods.*) What's he
been raving about now? Oh, what does it matter? He
makes me want to claw his hair out by the roots.
When I think of what you will be going through in a
few months' time—and all for him! It's as if you'd done
him wrong! These *men*! (*Turning on Cliff.*) And all the
time you just sit there, and do nothing!

CLIFF: (*looking up slowly*). That's right—I just sit here.

HELENA: What's the matter with you? What sort of a man are
you?

CLIFF: I'm not the District Commissioner, you know. Listen,
Helena—I don't feel like Jimmy does about you, but
I'm not exactly on your side either. And since you've
been here, everything's certainly been worse than it's
ever been. This has always been a battlefield, but I'm
pretty certain that if I hadn't been here, everything
would have been over between these two long ago. I've
been a—a no-man's land between them. Sometimes, it's
been still and peaceful, no incidents, and we've all been
reasonably happy. But most of the time, it's simply a
very narrow strip of plain hell. But where I come from,
we're used to brawling and excitement. Perhaps I even
enjoy being in the thick of it. I love these two people
very much. (*He looks at her steadily, and adds simply*)
And I pity all of us.

HELENA: Are you including me in that? (*But she goes on quickly
to avoid his reply.*) I don't understand him, you or any
of it. All I know is that none of you seems to know how
to behave in a decent, civilised way. (*In command now.*)
Listen, Alison—I've sent your father a wire.

ALISON: (*numbed and vague by now*). Oh?

Helena looks at her, and realizes quickly that everything now will have to depend on her own authority. She tries to explain patiently.

HELENA: Look, dear—he'll get it first thing in the morning. I thought it would be better than trying to explain the situation over the 'phone. I asked him to come up, and fetch you home tomorrow.

ALISON: What did you say?

HELENA: Simply that you wanted to come home, and would he come up for you.

ALISON: I see.

HELENA: I knew that would be quite enough. I told him there was nothing to worry about, so they won't worry and think there's been an accident or anything. I had to do something, dear. (*Very gently.*) You didn't mind, did you?

ALISON: No, I don't mind. Thank you.

HELENA: And you will go when he comes for you?

ALISON: (*Pause.*) Yes. I'll go.

HELENA: (*relieved*). I expect he'll drive up. He should be here about tea-time. It'll give you plenty of time to get your things together. And, perhaps, after you've gone— Jimmy (*saying the word almost with difficulty*) will come to his senses, and face up to things.

ALISON: Who was on the 'phone?

HELENA: I didn't catch it properly. It rang after I'd sent the wire off—just as soon as I put the receiver down almost. I had to go back down the stairs again. Sister somebody, I think.

ALISON: Must have been a hospital or something. Unless he knows someone in a convent—*that* doesn't seem very likely, does it? Well, we'll be late, if we don't hurry. (*She puts down one of the prayer books on the table.*) *Enter Jimmy. He comes down C., between the two women.*

CLIFF: All right, boyo?

JIMMY: (*to Alison*). It's Hugh's mum. She's—had a stroke. *Slight pause.*

61

ALISON: I'm sorry.

Jimmy sits on the bed.

CLIFF: How bad is it?

JIMMY: They didn't say much. But I think she's dying.

CLIFF: Oh dear. . . .

JIMMY: (*rubbing his fist over his face*). It doesn't make any sense at all. Do you think it does?

ALISON: I'm sorry—I really am.

CLIFF: Anything I can do?

JIMMY: The London train goes in half an hour. You'd better order me a taxi.

CLIFF: Right. (*He crosses to the door, and stops.*) Do you want me to come with you, boy?

JIMMY: No thanks. After all, you hardly knew her. It's not for you to go.

Helena looks quickly at Alison.

She may not even remember me, for all I know.

CLIFF: O.K.

EXIT.

JIMMY: I remember the first time I showed her your photograph—just after we were married. She looked at it, and the tears just welled up in her eyes, and she said: "But she's so beautiful! She's so beautiful!" She kept repeating it as if she couldn't believe it. Sounds a bit simple and sentimental when you repeat it. But it was pure gold the way she said it.

He looks at her. She is standing by the dressing table, her back to him.

She got a kick out of you, like she did out of everything else. Hand me my shoes, will you?

She kneels down, and hands them to him.

(*looking down at his feet*). You're coming with me, aren't you? She (*he shrugs*) hasn't got anyone else now. I . . . need you . . . to come with me.

He looks into her eyes, but she turns away, and stands up. Outside, the church bells start ringing. Helena moves up to the door, and waits watching them closely. Alison stands quite still, Jimmy's eyes burning into her. Then, she crosses

62

in front of him to the table where she picks up the prayer book, her back to him. She wavers, and seems about to say something, but turns upstage instead, and walks quickly to the door.

ALISON: (*hardly audible*). Let's go.

She goes out, Helena following. Jimmy gets up, looks about him unbelievingly, and leans against the chest of drawers. The teddy bear is close to his face, and he picks it up gently, looks at it quickly, and throws it downstage. It hits the floor with a thud, and it makes a rattling, groaning sound—as guaranteed in the advertisement. Jimmy falls forward on to the bed, his face buried in the covers.

QUICK CURTAIN

END OF SCENE I

ACT TWO

ACT II

SCENE TWO

The following evening. When the curtain rises, ALISON is discovered R., going from her dressing table to the bed, and packing her things into a suitcase. Sitting down L. is her father, COLONEL REDFERN, a large handsome man, about sixty. Forty years of being a soldier sometimes conceals the essentially gentle, kindly man underneath. Brought up to command respect, he is often slightly withdrawn and uneasy now that he finds himself in a world where his authority has lately become less and less unquestionable. His wife would relish the present situation, but he is only disturbed and bewildered by it. He looks around him, discreetly scrutinising everything.

63

COLONEL: (*partly to himself*). I'm afraid it's all beyond me. I suppose it always will be. As for Jimmy—he just speaks a different language from any of us. Where did you say he'd gone?

ALISON: He's gone to see Mrs. Tanner.

COLONEL: Who?

ALISON: Hugh Tanner's mother.

COLONEL: Oh, I see.

ALISON: She's been taken ill—a stroke. Hugh's abroad, as you know, so Jimmy's gone to London to see her.
He nods.
He wanted me to go with him.

COLONEL: Didn't she start him off in this sweet-stall business?

ALISON: Yes.

COLONEL: What is she like? Nothing like her son, I trust?

ALISON: Not remotely. Oh—how can you describe her? Rather —ordinary. What Jimmy insists on calling working class. A Charwoman who married an actor, worked hard all her life, and spent most of it struggling to support her husband and her son. Jimmy and she are very fond of each other.

COLONEL: So you didn't go with him?

ALISON: No.

COLONEL: Who's looking after the sweet-stall?

ALISON: Cliff. He should be in soon.

COLONEL: Oh yes, of course—Cliff. Does he live here too?

ALISON: Yes. His room is just across the landing.

COLONEL: Sweet-stall. It does seem an extraordinary thing for an educated young man to be occupying himself with. Why should he want to do that, of all things. I've always thought he must be quite clever in his way.

ALISON: (*no longer interested in this problem*). Oh, he tried so many things—journalism, advertising, even vacuum cleaners for a few weeks. He seems to have been as happy doing this as anything else.

COLONEL: I've often wondered what it was like—where you were living, I mean. You didn't tell us very much in your letters.

64

ALISON: There wasn't a great deal to tell you. There's not much social life here.

COLONEL: Oh, I know what you mean. You were afraid of being disloyal to your husband.

ALISON: Disloyal! (*She laughs.*) He thought it was high treason of me to write to you at all! I used to have to dodge downstairs for the post, so that he wouldn't see I was getting letters from home. Even then I had to hide them.

COLONEL: He really does hate us doesn't he?

ALISON: Oh yes—don't have any doubts about that. He hates all of us.

COLONEL: (*sighs*). It seems a great pity. It was all so unfortunate —unfortunate and unnecessary. I'm afraid I can't help feeling that he must have had a certain amount of right on his side.

ALISON: (*puzzled by this admission*). Right on his side?

COLONEL: It's a little late to admit it, I know, but your mother and I weren't entirely free from blame. I have never said anything—there was no point afterwards—but I have always believed that she went too far over Jimmy. Of course, she was extremely upset at the time—we both were—and that explains a good deal of what happened. I did my best to stop her, but she was in such a state of mind, there was simply nothing I could do. She seemed to have made up her mind that if he was going to marry you, he must be a criminal, at the very least. All those inquiries, the private detectives— the accusations. I hated every moment of it.

ALISON: I suppose she was trying to protect me—in a rather heavy-handed way, admittedly.

COLONEL: I must confess I find that kind of thing rather horrifying. Anyway, I try to think now that it never happened. I didn't approve of Jimmy at all, and I don't suppose I ever should, but, looking back on it, I think it would have been better, for all concerned, if we had never attempted to interfere. At least, it would have been a little more dignified.

ALISON: It wasn't your fault.

COLONEL: I don't know. We were all to blame, in our different ways. No doubt Jimmy acted in good faith. He's honest enough, whatever else he may be. And your mother—in her heavy-handed way, as you put it—acted in good faith as well. Perhaps you and I were the ones most to blame.

ALISON: You and I!

COLONEL: I think you may take after me a little, my dear. You like to sit on the fence because it's comfortable and more peaceful.

ALISON: Sitting on the fence! I married him, didn't I.

COLONEL: Oh yes, you did.

ALISON: In spite of all the humiliating scenes and the threats! What did you say to me at the time? Wasn't I letting you down, turning against you, how could I do this to you etcetera?

COLONEL: Perhaps it might have been better if you hadn't written letters to us—knowing how we felt about your husband, and after everything that had happened. (*He looks at her uncomfortably.*) Forgive me, I'm a little confused, what with everything—the telegram, driving up here suddenly. . . .

He trails off rather helplessly. He looks tired. He glances at her nervously, a hint of accusation in his eyes, as if he expected her to defend herself further. She senses this, and is more confused than ever.

ALISON: Do you know what he said about Mummy? He said she was an overfed, overprivileged old bitch. "A good blow-out for the worms" was his expression, I think.

COLONEL: I see. And what does he say about me?

ALISON: Oh, he doesn't seem to mind you so much. In fact, I think he rather likes you. He likes you because he can feel sorry for you. (*Conscious that what she says is going to hurt him.*) "Poor old Daddy—just one of those sturdy old plants left over from the Edwardian Wilderness that can't understand why the sun isn't

66

shining any more." (*Rather lamely.*) Something like
that, anyway.

COLONEL: He has quite a turn of phrase, hasn't he? (*Simply, and
without malice.*) Why did you ever have to meet this
young man?

ALISON: Oh, Daddy, please don't put me on trial now. I've been
on trial every day and night of my life for nearly four
years.

COLONEL: But why should he have married you, feeling as he did
about everything?

ALISON: That is the famous American question—you know, the
sixty-four dollar one! Perhaps it was revenge.
He looks up uncomprehendingly.
Oh yes. Some people do actually marry for revenge.
People like Jimmy, anyway. Or perhaps he should have
been another Shelley, and can't understand now why
I'm not another Mary, and you're not William
Godwin. He thinks he's got a sort of genius for love
and friendship—on his own terms. Well, for twenty
years, I'd lived a happy, uncomplicated life, and
suddenly, this—this spiritual barbarian—throws down
the gauntlet at me. Perhaps only another woman could
understand what a challenge like that means—although
I think Helena was as mystified as you are.

COLONEL: I am mystified. (*He rises, and crosses to the window R.*).
Your husband has obviously taught you a great deal,
whether you realise it or not. What any of it means, I
don't know. I always believed that people married each
other because they were in love. That always seemed a
good enough reason to me. But apparently, that's too
simple for young people nowadays. They have to talk
about challenges and revenge. I just can't believe that
love between men and women is really like that.

ALISON: Only some men and women.

COLONEL: But why you? My daughter. . . . No. Perhaps Jimmy is
right. Perhaps I am a—what was it? an old plant left
over from the Edwardian Wilderness. And I can't
understand why the sun isn't shining any more. You

can see what he means, can't you? It was March, 1914, when I left England, and, apart from leaves every ten years or so, I didn't see much of my own country until we all came back in '47. Oh, I knew things had changed, of course. People told you all the time the way it was going—going to the dogs, as the Blimps are supposed to say. But it seemed very unreal to me, out there. The England I remembered was the one I left in 1914, and I was happy to go on remembering it that way. Beside, I had the Maharajah's army to command—that was my world, and I loved it, all of it. At the time, it looked like going on forever. When I think of it now, it seems like a dream. If only it could have gone on forever. Those long, cool evenings up in the hills, everything purple and golden. Your mother and I were so happy then. It seemed as though we had everything we could ever want. I think the last day the sun shone was when that dirty little train steamed out of that crowded, suffocating Indian station, and the battalion band playing for all it was worth. I knew in my heart it was all over then. Everything.

ALISON: You're hurt because everything is changed. Jimmy is hurt because everything is the same. And neither of you can face it. Something's gone wrong somewhere, hasn't it?

COLONEL: It looks like it, my dear.

She picks up the squirrel from the chest of drawers, is about to put it in her suitcase, hesitates, and then puts it back. The Colonel turns and looks at her. She moves down towards him, her head turned away. For a few moments, she seems to be standing on the edge of choice. The choice made, her body wheels round suddenly, and she is leaning against him, weeping softly.

(*presently*). This is a big step you're taking. You've made up your mind to come back with me? Is that really what you want?

Enter Helena.

HELENA: I'm sorry. I came in to see if I could help you pack,

Alison. Oh, you look as though you've finished.
*Alison leaves her father, and moves to the bed, pushing
down the lid of her suitcase.*

ALISON: All ready.

HELENA: Have you got everything?

ALISON: Well, no. But Cliff can send the rest on sometime, I
expect. He should have been back by now. Oh, of
course, he's had to put the stall away on his own
today.

COLONEL: (*crossing and picking up the suitcase*). Well, I'd better
put this in the car then. We may as well get along.
Your mother will be worried, I know. I promised her
I'd ring her when I got here. She's not very well.

HELENA: I hope my telegram didn't upset her too much. Perhaps
I shouldn't have——

COLONEL: Not at all. We were very grateful that you did. It was
very kind of you, indeed. She tried to insist on coming
with me, but I finally managed to talk her out of it. I
thought it would be best for everyone. What about your
case, Helena? If you care to tell me where it is, I'll take
it down with this one.

HELENA: I'm afraid I shan't be coming tonight.

ALISON: (*very surprised*). Aren't you coming with us?
Enter Cliff.

HELENA: I'd like to, but the fact is I've an appointment
tomorrow in Birmingham—about a job. They've just
sent me a script. It's rather important, and I don't
want to miss it. So it looks as though I shall have to
stay here tonight.

ALISON: Oh, I see. Hullo, Cliff.

CLIFF: Hullo there.

ALISON: Daddy—this is Cliff.

COLONEL: How do you do, Cliff.

CLIFF: How do you do, sir.
Slight pause.

COLONEL: Well, I'd better put this in the car, hadn't I? Don't
be long, Alison. Good-bye, Helena. I expect we shall
be seeing you again soon, if you're not busy.

HELENA: Oh, yes, I shall be back in a day or two.
Cliff takes off his jacket.

COLONEL: Well, then—good-bye, Cliff.

CLIFF: Good-bye, sir.
The Colonel goes out. Cliff comes down L. Helena moves C.
You're really going then?

ALISON: Really going.

CLIFF: I should think Jimmy would be back pretty soon. You won't wait?

ALISON: No, Cliff.

CLIFF: Who's going to tell him?

HELENA: I can tell him. That is, if I'm here when he comes back.

CLIFF: (*quietly*). You'll be here. (*To Alison.*) Don't you think you ought to tell him yourself?
She hands him an envelope from her handbag. He takes it.
Bit conventional, isn't it?

ALISON: I'm a conventional girl.
He crosses to her, and puts his arms round her.

CLIFF: (*back over his shoulder, to Helena*). I hope you're right, that's all.

HELENA: What do you mean? You hope *I'm* right?

CLIFF: (*to Alison*). The place is going to be really cock-eyed now. You know that, don't you?

ALISON: Please, Cliff——
He nods. She kisses him.
I'll write to you later.

CLIFF: Good-bye, lovely.

ALISON: Look after him.

CLIFF: We'll keep the old nut-house going somehow.
She crosses C., in between the two of them, glances quickly at the two armchairs, the papers still left around them from yesterday. Helena kisses her on the cheek, and squeezes her hand.

HELENA: See you soon.
Alison nods, and goes out quickly. Cliff and Helena are left looking at each other.

70

Would you like me to make you some tea?

CLIFF: No, thanks.

HELENA: Think I might have some myself, if you don't mind.

CLIFF: So you're staying?

HELENA: Just for tonight. Do you object?

CLIFF: Nothing to do with me. (*Against the table C.*) Of course, he may not be back until later on.

She crosses L., to the window, and lights a cigarette.

HELENA: What do you think he'll do? Perhaps he'll look out one of his old girl friends. What about this Madeline?

CLIFF: What about her?

HELENA: Isn't she supposed to have done a lot for him? Couldn't he go back to her?

CLIFF: I shouldn't think so.

HELENA: What happened ?

CLIFF: She was nearly old enough to be his mother. I expect that's something to do with it! Why the hell should I know!

For the first time in the play, his good humour has completely deserted him. She looks surprised.

HELENA: You're his friend, aren't you? Anyway, he's not what you'd call reticent about himself, is he? I've never seen so many souls stripped to the waist since I've been here.

He turns to go.

HELENA: Aren't you staying?

CLIFF: No, I'm not. There was a train in from London about five minutes ago. And, just in case he may have been on it, I'm going out.

HELENA: Don't you think you ought to be here when he comes?

CLIFF: I've had a hard day, and I don't think I want to see anyone hurt until I've had something to eat first, and perhaps a few drinks as well. I think I might pick up some nice, pleasant little tart in a milk bar, and sneak her in past old mother Drury. Here! (*Tossing the letter at her.*) You give it to him! (*Crossing to door.*) He's all yours. (*At door.*) And I hope he rams it up your nostrils!

EXIT.

*She crosses to the table, and stubs out her cigarette. The
front door downstairs is heard to slam. She moves to the
wardrobe, opens it idly. It is empty, except for one dress,
swinging on a hanger. She goes over to the dressing table,
now cleared but for a framed photograph of Jimmy. Idly,
she slams the empty drawers open and shut. She turns
upstage to the chest of drawers, picks up the toy bear, and
sits on the bed, looking at it. She lays her head back on
the pillow, still holding the bear. She looks up quickly as
the door crashes open, and Jimmy enters. He stands
looking at her, then moves down C., taking off his raincoat,
and throwing it over the table. He is almost giddy with
anger, and has to steady himself on the chair. He looks
up.*

JIMMY: That old bastard nearly ran me down in his car! Now,
if he'd killed me, that really would have been ironical.
And how right and fitting that my wife should have
been a passenger. A passenger! What's the matter with
everybody? (*Crossing up to her.*) Cliff practically walked
into me, coming out of the house. He belted up the
other way, and pretended not to see me. Are you the
only one who's not afraid to stay?
She hands him Alison's note. He takes it.
Oh, it's one of these, is it? (*He rips it open.*)
He reads a few lines, and almost snorts with disbelief.
Did you write this for her! Well, listen to this then!
(*Reading.*) "My dear—I must get away. I don't suppose
you will understand, but please try. I need peace so
desperately, and, at the moment, I am willing to
sacrifice everything just for that. I don't know what's
going to happen to us. I know you will be feeling
wretched and bitter, but try to be a little patient with
me. I shall always have a deep, loving need of you—
Alison". Oh, how could she be so bloody wet! Deep
loving need! That makes me puke! (*Crossing to R.*)
She couldn't say "You rotten bastard! I hate your guts,
I'm clearing out, and I hope you rot!" No, she has to
make a polite, emotional mess out of it! (*Seeing the dress*

72

in the wardrobe, he rips it out, and throws it in the corner up L.) Deep, loving need! I never thought she was capable of being as phoney as that! What is that—a line from one of those plays you've been in? What are you doing here anyway? You'd better keep out of my way, if you don't want your head kicked in.

HELENA: (*calmly*). If you'll stop thinking about yourself for one moment, I'll tell you something I think you ought to know. Your wife is going to have a baby.

He just looks at her.

Well? Doesn't that mean anything? Even to you?

He is taken aback, but not so much by the news, as by her.

JIMMY: All right—yes. I am surprised. I give you that. But, tell me. Did you honestly expect me to go soggy at the knees, and collapse with remorse! (*Leaning nearer.*) Listen, if you'll stop breathing your female wisdom all over me, I'll tell you something: I don't care. (*Beginning quietly.*) I don't care if she's going to have a baby. I don't care if it has two heads! (*He knows her fingers are itching.*) Do I disgust you? Well, go on—slap my face. But remember what I told you before, will you? For eleven hours, I have been watching someone I love very much going through the sordid process of dying. She was alone, and I was the only one with her. And when I have to walk behind that coffin on Thursday, I'll be on my own again. Because that bitch won't even send her a bunch of flowers—I know! She made the great mistake of all her kind. She thought that because Hugh's mother was a deprived and ignorant old woman, who said all the wrong things in all the wrong places, she couldn't be taken seriously. And you think I should be overcome with awe because that cruel, stupid girl is going to have a baby! (*Anguish in his voice.*) I can't believe it! I can't. (*Grabbing her shoulder.*) Well, the performance is over. Now leave me alone, and *get out*, you evil-minded little virgin.

She slaps his face savagely. An expression of horror and

73

disbelief floods his face. But it drains away, and all that is left is pain. His hand goes up to his head, and a muffled cry of despair escapes him. Helena tears his hand away, and kisses him passionately, drawing him down beside her.

CURTAIN

END OF ACT II

ACT III

SCENE ONE

Several months later. A Sunday evening. ALISON'S
personal belongings, such as her make-up things on the
dressing table, for example, have been replaced by
HELENA'S.

AT RISE of curtain, we find JIMMY and CLIFF sprawled in
their respective armchairs, immersed in the Sunday
newspapers. HELENA is standing down L. leaning over
the ironing board, a small pile of clothes beside her.
She looks more attractive than before, for the setting of
her face is more relaxed. She still looks quite smart, but
in an unpremeditated, careless way; she wears an old
shirt of JIMMY'S.

CLIFF: That stinking old pipe!
Pause.
JIMMY: Shut up.
CLIFF: Why don't you do something with it?
JIMMY: Why do I spend half of Sunday reading the papers?
CLIFF: (*kicks him without lowering his paper*). It stinks!
JIMMY: So do you, but I'm not singing an aria about it.
(*Turns to the next page.*) The dirty ones get more and
more wet round the mouth, and the posh ones are
more pompous than ever. (*Lowering paper, and waving
pipe at Helena.*) Does this bother you?
HELENA: No. I quite like it.
JIMMY: (*to Cliff*). There you are—she likes it!
He returns to his paper. Cliff grunts.
Have you read about the grotesque and evil practices
going on in the Midlands?
CLIFF: Read about the what?

JIMMY: Grotesque and evil practices going on in the Midlands.

CLIFF: No, what about 'em?

JIMMY: Seems we don't know the old place. It's all in here. Startling Revelations this week! Pictures too. Reconstructions of midnight invocations to the Coptic Goddess of fertility.

HELENA: Sounds madly depraved.

JIMMY: Yes, it's rather us, isn't it? My gosh, look at 'em! Snarling themselves silly. Next week a well-known debutante relates how, during an evil orgy in Market Harborough, she killed and drank the blood of a white cockerel. Well—I'll bet Fortnums must be doing a roaring line in sacrificial cocks! (*Thoughtful.*) Perhaps that's what Miss Drury does on Sunday evenings. She puts in a stint as evil high priestess down at the Y.W.—probably having a workout at this very moment. (*To Helena.*) You never dabbled in this kind of thing, did you?

HELENA: (*laughs*). Not lately!

JIMMY: Sounds rather your cup of tea—cup of blood, I should say. (*In an imitation of a midlands accent.*) Well, I mean, it gives you something to do, doesn't it? After all, it wouldn't do if we was all alike, would it? It'd be a funny world if we was all the same, that's what *I* always say! (*Resuming in his normal voice.*) All I know is that somebody's been sticking pins into *my* wax image for years. (*Suddenly.*) Of course: Alison's mother! Every Friday, the wax arrives from Harrods, and all through the week-end, she's stabbing away at it with a hatpin! Ruined her bridge game, I dare say.

HELENA: Why don't *you* try it?

JIMMY: Yes, it's an idea. (*Pointing to Cliff.*) Just for a start, we could roast him over the gas stove. Have we got enough shillings for the meter? It seems to be just the thing for these Autumn evenings. After all the whole point of a sacrifice is that you give up something you never really wanted in the first place. You know what I mean? People are doing it around you all the time. They give

76

up their careers, say—or their beliefs—or sex. And everyone thinks to themselves: how wonderful to be able to do that. If only I were capable of doing that! But the truth of it is that they've been kidding themselves, and they've been kidding you. It's not awfully difficult—giving up something you were incapable of ever really wanting. We shouldn't be admiring them. We should feel rather sorry for them. (*Coming back from this sudden, brooding excursion, and turning to Cliff.*) You'll make an admirable sacrifice.

CLIFF: (*mumbling*). Dry up! I'm trying to read.

JIMMY: Afterwards, we can make a loving cup from his blood. Can't say I fancy that so much. I've seen it—it looks like cochineal, ever so common. (*To Helena.*) Yours would be much better—pale Cambridge blue, I imagine. No? And afterwards, we could make invocations to the Coptic Goddess of fertility. Got any idea how you do that? (*To Cliff.*) Do you know?

CLIFF: Shouldn't have thought *you* needed to make invocations to the Coptic whatever-she-is!

JIMMY: Yes, I see what you mean. (*To Helena.*) Well, we don't want to *ask* for trouble, do we? Perhaps it might appeal to the lady here—she's written a long letter all about artificial insemination. It's headed: Haven't we tried God's patience enough! (*Throws the paper down.*) Let's see the other posh one.

CLIFF: Haven't finished yet.

JIMMY: Well, hurry up. I'll have to write and ask them to put hyphens in between the syllables for you. There's a particularly savage correspondence going on in there about whether Milton wore braces or not. I just want to see who gets shot down this week.

CLIFF: Just read that. Don't know what it was about, but a Fellow of All Souls seems to have bitten the dust, and the Athenaeum's going up in flames, so the Editor declares that this correspondence is now closed.

JIMMY: I think you're actually acquiring yourself a curiosity, my boy. Oh yes, and then there's an American professor

77

from Yale or somewhere, who believes that when
Shakespeare was writing *The Tempest*, he changed his
sex. Yes, he was obliged to go back to Stratford because
the other actors couldn't take him seriously any longer.
This professor chap is coming over here to search for
certain documents which will prove that poor old W.S.
ended up in someone else's second best bed—a certain
Warwickshire farmer's, whom he married after having
three children by him.

Helena laughs. Jimmy looks up quizzically.
Is anything the matter?

HELENA: No, nothing. I'm only beginning to get used to him. I
never (*this is to Cliff*) used to be sure when he was
being serious, or when he wasn't.

CLIFF: Don't think he knows himself half the time. When in
doubt, just mark it down as an insult.

JIMMY: Hurry up with that paper, and shut up! What are we
going to do tonight? There isn't even a decent concert
on. (*To Helena.*) Are you going to Church?

HELENA: (*rather taken aback*). No. I don't think so. Unless you
want to.

JIMMY: Do I detect a growing, satanic glint in her eyes lately?
Do you think it's living in sin with me that does it?
(*To Helena.*) Do you feel very sinful my dear? Well?
Do you?

*She can hardly believe that this is an attack, and she can
only look at him, uncertain of herself.*

Do you feel sin crawling out of your ears, like stored
up wax or something? Are you wondering whether I'm
joking or not? Perhaps I ought to wear a red nose and
funny hat. I'm just curious, that's all.

*She is shaken by the sudden coldness in his eyes, but
before she has time to fully realise how hurt she is, he is
smiling at her, and shouting cheerfully at Cliff.*

Let's have that paper, stupid!

CLIFF: Why don't you drop dead!

JIMMY: (*to Helena*). Will you be much longer doing that?

HELENA: Nearly finished.

78

JIMMY: Talking of sin, wasn't that Miss Drury's Reverend friend I saw you chatting with yesterday. Helena darling, I said wasn't that. . . .

HELENA: Yes it was.

JIMMY: My dear, you don't have to be on the defensive you know.

HELENA: I'm not on the defensive.

JIMMY: After all, there's no reason why we shouldn't have the parson to tea up here. Why don't we? Did you find that you had much in common?

HELENA: No I don't think so.

JIMMY: Do you think that some of this spiritual beefcake would make a man of me? Should I go in for this moral weight lifting and get myself some over-developed muscle? I was a liberal skinny weakling. I too was afraid to strip down to my soul, but now everyone looks at my superb physique in envy. I can perform any kind of press there is without betraying the least sign of passion or kindliness.

HELENA: All right Jimmy.

JIMMY: Two years ago I couldn't even lift up my head—now I have more uplift than a film starlet.

HELENA: Jimmy, can we have one day, just one day, without tumbling over religion or politics?

CLIFF: Yes, change the record old boy, or pipe down.

JIMMY: (*rising*). Thought of the title for a new song today. It's called "My mother's in the madhouse—that's why I'm in love with you." The lyrics are catchy too. I was thinking we might work it into the act.

HELENA: Good idea.

JIMMY: I was thinking we'd scrub Jock and Day, and call ourselves something else. "And jocund day stands tiptoed on the misty mountain tops." It's too intellectual! Anyway, I shouldn't think people will want to be reminded of that peculiar man's plays after Harvard and Yale have finished with him. How about something bright and snappy? I know—— What about—T. S. Eliot and Pam!

CLIFF: (*casually falling in with this familiar routine*). Mirth, mellerdy and madness!

JIMMY: (*sitting at the table R. and "strumming" it*). Bringing quips and strips for you!
They sing together.
"For we may be guilty, darling. . . .
But we're both insane as well!"
Jimmy stands up, and rattles his lines off at almost unintelligible speed.
Ladies and gentlemen, as I was coming to the theatre tonight, I was passing through the stage door, and a man comes up to me, and 'e says:

CLIFF: 'Ere! Have you seen nobody?

JIMMY: Have I seen who?

CLIFF: Have you seen nobody?

JIMMY: Of course, I haven't seen nobody! Kindly don't waste my time! Ladies and gentlemen, a little recitation entitled "She said she was called a little Gidding, but she was more like a gelding iron!" Thank you "She said she was called little Gidding——"

CLIFF: Are you quite sure you haven't seen nobody?

JIMMY: Are you still here?

CLIFF: I'm looking for nobody!

JIMMY: *Will* you kindly go away! "She said she was called little Gidding——"

CLIFF: Well, I can't find nobody anywhere, and I'm supposed to give him this case!

JIMMY: Will you kindly stop interrupting per*lease*! Can't you see I'm trying to entertain these ladies and gentlemen? Who is this nobody you're talking about?

CLIFF: I was told to come here and give this case to nobody.

JIMMY: You were told to come here and give this case to nobody.

CLIFF: That's right. And when I gave it to him, nobody would give me a shilling.

JIMMY: And when you gave it to him, nobody would give you a shilling.

CLIFF: That's right.

JIMMY: Well, what about it?

CLIFF: Nobody's not here!

JIMMY: Now, let me get this straight: when you say nobody's here, you don't mean nobody's here?

CLIFF: No.

JIMMY: No.

JIMMY: You mean—nobody's here.

CLIFF: That's right.

JIMMY: Well, why didn't you say so before?

HELENA: (*not quite sure if this is really her cue*). Hey! You down there!

JIMMY: Oh, it goes on for hours yet, but never mind. What is it, sir?

HELENA: (*shouting*). I think your sketch stinks! I say—I think your sketch stinks!

JIMMY: He thinks it stinks. And, who, pray, might you be?

HELENA: Me? Oh—(*with mock modesty*) I'm nobody.

JIMMY: Then here's your bloody case!

He hurls a cushion at her, which hits the ironing board.

HELENA: My ironing board!

The two men do a Flanagan and Allen, moving slowly in step, as they sing.

> Now there's a certain little lady, and you all know
> who I mean,
> She may have been to Roedean, but to me she's
> still a queen.
> Someday I'm goin' to marry her,
> When times are not so bad,
> Her mother doesn't care for me
> So I'll 'ave to ask 'er dad.
> We'll build a little home for two,
> And have some quiet menage,
> We'll send our kids to public school
> And live on bread and marge.
> Don't be afraid to sleep with your sweetheart,
> Just because she's better than you.
> Those forgotten middle-classes may have fallen on
> their noses,

But a girl who's true blue,
Will still have something left for you,
The angels up above, will know that you're in love
So don't be afraid to sleep with your sweetheart,
Just because she's better than you. . . .
        They call me Sydney,
Just because she's better than you.

But Jimmy has had enough of this gag by now, and he pushes Cliff away.

JIMMY: Your damned great feet! That's the second time you've kicked my ankle! It's no good—Helena will have to do it. Go on, go and make some tea, and we'll decide what we're going to do.

CLIFF: Make some yourself!

He pushes him back violently, Jimmy loses his balance, and falls over.

JIMMY: You rough bastard!

He leaps up, and they grapple, falling on to the floor with a crash. They roll about, grunting and gasping. Cliff manages to kneel on Jimmy's chest.

CLIFF: (*breathing heavily*). I want to read the papers!

JIMMY: You're a savage, a hooligan! You really are! Do you know that! You don't deserve to live in the same house with decent, sensitive people!

CLIFF: Are you going to dry up, or do I read the papers down here?

Jimmy makes a supreme effort, and Cliff topples to the floor.

JIMMY: You've made me wrench my guts!

He pushes the struggling Cliff down.

CLIFF: Look what you're doing! You're ripping my shirt. Get *off*!

JIMMY: Well, what do you want to wear a shirt for? (*Rising.*) A tough character like you! Now go and make me some tea.

CLIFF: It's the only clean one I've got. Oh, you big oaf! (*Getting up from the floor, and appealing to Helena.*) Look! It's filthy!

82

HELENA: Yes, it is. He's stronger than he looks. If you like to take it off now, I'll wash it through for you. It'll be dry by the time we want to go out.

Cliff hesitates.

What's the matter, Cliff?

CLIFF: Oh, it'll be all right.

JIMMY: Give it to her, and quit moaning!

CLIFF: Oh, all right.

He takes it off, and gives it to her.

Thanks, Helena.

HELENA: (*taking it*). Right. I won't be a minute with it.

She goes out. Jimmy flops into his armchair. R.

JIMMY: (*amused*). You look like Marlon Brando or something. (*Slight pause.*) You don't care for Helena, do you?

CLIFF: You didn't seem very keen yourself once. (*Hesitating, then quickly.*) It's not the same, is it?

JIMMY: (*irritably*). No, of course it's not the same, you idiot! It never is! Today's meal is always different from yesterday's and the last woman isn't the same as the one before. If you can't accept that, you're going to be pretty unhappy, my boy.

CLIFF: (*sits on the arm of his chair, and rubs his feet*). Jimmy—I don't think I shall stay here much longer.

JIMMY: (*rather casually*). Oh, why not?

CLIFF: (*picking up his tone*). Oh, I don't know. I've just thought of trying somewhere different. The sweet-stall's all right, but I think I'd like to try something else. You're highly educated, and it suits you, but I need something a bit better.

JIMMY: Just as you like, my dear boy. It's your business, not mine.

CLIFF: And another thing—I think Helena finds it rather a lot of work to do with two chaps about the place. It won't be so much for her if there's just the two of you. Anyway, I think I ought to find some girl who'll just look after me.

JIMMY: Sounds like a good idea. Can't think who'd be stupid enough to team themselves up with you though.

83

Perhaps Helena can think of somebody for you—one
of her posh girl friends with lots of money, and no
brains. That's what you want.

CLIFF: Something like that.

JIMMY: Any idea what you're going to do?

CLIFF: Not much.

JIMMY: That sounds like you all right! Shouldn't think you'll
last five minutes without me to explain the score to you.

CLIFF: (*grinning*). Don't suppose so.

JIMMY: You're such a scruffy little beast—I'll bet some
respectable little madam from Pinner or Guildford
gobbles you up in six months. She'll marry you, send
you out to work, and you'll end up as clean as a new
pin.

CLIFF: (*chuckling*). Yes, I'm stupid enough for that too!

JIMMY: (*to himself*). I seem to spend my life saying good-bye.
Slight pause.

CLIFF: My feet hurt.

JIMMY: Try washing your socks. (*Slowly.*) It's a funny thing.
You've been loyal, generous and a good friend. But I'm
quite prepared to see you wander off, find a new home,
and make out on your own. And all because of something I want from that girl downstairs, something I
know in my heart she's incapable of giving. You're
worth a half a dozen Helenas to me or to anyone. And,
if you were in my place, you'd do the same thing.
Right?

CLIFF: Right.

JIMMY: Why, why, why, why do we let these women bleed us
to death? Have you ever had a letter, and on it is
franked "Please Give Your Blood Generously"? Well,
the Postmaster-General does that, on behalf of all the
women of the world. I suppose people of our generation
aren't able to die for good causes any longer. We had
all that done for us, in the thirties and the forties, when
we were still kids. (*In his familiar, semi-serious mood.*)
There aren't any good, brave causes left. If the big
bang does come, and we all get killed off, it won't be in

84

aid of the old-fashioned, grand design. It'll just be for the Brave New-nothing-very-much-thank-you. About as pointless and inglorious as stepping in front of a bus. No, there's nothing left for it, me boy, but to let yourself be butchered by the women.

Enter Helena.

HELENA: Here you are, Cliff. (*Handing him the shirt.*)

CLIFF: Oh, thanks, Helena, very much. That's decent of you.

HELENA: Not at all. I should dry it over the gas—the fire in your room would be better. There won't be much room for it over that stove.

CLIFF: Right, I will. (*Crosses to door.*)

JIMMY: And hurry up about it, stupid. We'll all go out, and have a drink soon. (*To Helena.*) O.K.?

HELENA: O.K.

JIMMY: (*shouting to Cliff on his way out*). But make me some tea first, you madcap little Charlie.

She crosses down L.

JIMMY: Darling, I'm sick of seeing you behind that damned ironing board!

HELENA: (*wryly*). Sorry.

JIMMY: Get yourself glammed up, and we'll hit the town. See you've put a shroud over Mummy, I think you should have laid a Union Jack over it.

HELENA: Is anything wrong?

JIMMY: Oh, don't frown like that—you look like the presiding magistrate!

HELENA: How should I look?

JIMMY: As if your heart stirred a little when you looked at me.

HELENA: Oh, it does that all right.

JIMMY: Cliff tells me he's leaving us.

HELENA: I know. He told me last night.

JIMMY: Did he? I always seem to be at the end of the queue when they're passing information out.

HELENA: I'm sorry he's going.

JIMMY: Yes, so am I. He's a sloppy, irritating bastard, but he's got a big heart. You can forgive somebody almost anything for that. He's had to learn how to take it, and

85

he knows how to hand it out. Come here.

He is sitting on the arm of his chair. She crosses to him, and they look at each other. Then she puts out her hand, and runs it over his head, fondling his ear and neck.

Right from that first night, you have always put out your hand to me first. As if you expected nothing, or worse than nothing, and didn't care. You made a good enemy, didn't you? What they call a worthy opponent. But then, when people put down their weapons, it doesn't mean they've necessarily stopped fighting.

HELENA: *(steadily).* I love you.

JIMMY: I think perhaps you do. Yes, I think perhaps you do. Perhaps it means something to lie with your victorious general in your arms. Especially, when he's heartily sick of the whole campaign, tired out, hungry and dry. *His lips find her fingers, and he kisses them. She presses his head against her.*

You stood up, and came out to meet me. Oh, Helena— *His face comes up to hers, and they embrace fiercely.* Don't let anything go wrong!

HELENA: *(softly).* Oh, my darling——

JIMMY: Either you're with me or against me.

HELENA: I've always wanted you—always!

They kiss again.

JIMMY: T. S. Eliot and Pam, we'll make a good double. If you'll help me. I'll close that damned sweet-stall, and we'll start everything from scratch. What do you say? We'll get away from this place.

HELENA: *(nodding happily).* I say that's wonderful.

JIMMY: *(kissing her quickly).* Put all that junk away, and we'll get out. We'll get pleasantly, joyfully tiddly, we'll gaze at each other tenderly and lecherously in "The Builder's Arms", and then we'll come back here, and I'll make such love to you, you'll not care about anything else at all.

She moves away L., after kissing his hand.

HELENA: I'll just change out of your old shirt. *(Folding ironing board.)*

JIMMY: (*moving U.S. to door*). Right. I'll hurry up the little
man.
*But before he reaches the door, it opens and Alison
enters. She wears a raincoat, her hair is untidy, and she
looks rather ill. There is a stunned pause.*
ALISON: (*quietly*). Hullo.
JIMMY: (*to Helena, after a moment*). Friend of yours to see you.
*He goes out quickly, and the two women are left looking
at each other.*

QUICK CURTAIN

END OF SCENE ONE

ACT III

ACT III

SCENE TWO

It is a few minutes later. From CLIFF'S room, across the
landing, comes the sound of JIMMY'S jazz trumpet.
AT RISE of the Curtain, HELENA is standing L. of the
table, pouring out a cup of tea. ALISON is sitting on
the armchair R. She bends down and picks up
JIMMY'S pipe. Then she scoops up a little pile of ash
from the floor, and drops it in the ashtray on the arm
of the chair.

ALISON: He still smokes this foul old stuff. I used to hate it at
first, but you get used to it.
HELENA: Yes.
ALISON: I went to the pictures last week, and some old man
was smoking it in front, a few rows away. I actually
got up, and sat right behind him.

87

HELENA: (*coming down with cup of tea*). Here, have this. It usually seems to help.

ALISON: (*taking it*). Thanks.

HELENA: Are you sure you feel all right now?

ALISON: (*nods*). It was just—oh, everything. It's my own fault—entirely. I must be mad, coming here like this. I'm sorry, Helena.

HELENA: Why should you be sorry—you of all people?

ALISON: Because it was unfair and cruel of me to come back. I'm afraid a sense of timing is one of the things I seem to have learnt from Jimmy. But it's something that can be in very bad taste. (*Sips her tea.*) So many times, I've just managed to stop myself coming here—right at the last moment. Even today, when I went to the booking office at St. Pancras, it was like a charade, and I never believed that I'd let myself walk on to that train. And when I was on it, I got into a panic. I felt like a criminal. I told myself I'd turn round at the other end, and come straight back. I couldn't even believe that this place existed any more. But once I got here, there was nothing I could do. I had to convince myself that everything I remembered about this place had really happened to me once.

She lowers her cup, and her foot plays with the newspapers on the floor.

How many times in these past few months I've thought of the evenings we used to spend here in this room. Suspended and rather remote. You make a good cup of tea.

HELENA: (*sitting L. of table*). Something Jimmy taught *me*.

ALISON: (*covering her face*). Oh, why am I here! You must all wish me a thousand miles away!

HELENA: I don't wish anything of the kind. You've more right to be here than I.

ALISON: Oh, Helena, don't bring out the book of rules——

HELENA: You are his wife, aren't you? Whatever I have done, I've never been able to forget that fact. You have all the rights——

88

ALISON: Helena—even I gave up believing in the divine rights of marriage long ago. Even before I met Jimmy. They've got something different now—constitutional monarchy. You are where you are by consent. And if you start trying any strong arm stuff, you're out. And I'm out.

HELENA: Is that something you learnt from him?

ALISON: Don't make me feel like a blackmailer or something, please! I've done something foolish, and rather vulgar in coming here tonight. I regret it, and I detest myself for doing it. But I did not come here in order to gain anything. Whatever it was—hysteria or just macabre curiosity, I'd certainly no intention of making any kind of breach between you and Jimmy. You must believe that.

HELENA: Oh, I believe it all right. That's why everything seems more wrong and terrible than ever. You didn't even reproach me. You should have been outraged, but you weren't. (*She leans back, as if she wanted to draw back from herself.*) I feel so—*ashamed*.

ALISON: You talk as though he were something you'd swindled me out of——

HELENA: (*fiercely*). And you talk as if he were a book or something you pass around to anyone who happens to want it for five minutes. What's the matter with you? You sound as though you were quoting *him* all the time. I thought you told me once you couldn't bring yourself to believe in him.

ALISON: I don't think I ever believed in your way either.

HELENA: At least, I still believe in right and wrong! Not even the months in this madhouse have stopped me doing that. Even though everything I have done is wrong, at least I have known it was wrong.

ALISON: You loved him, didn't you? That's what you wrote, and told me.

HELENA: And it was true.

ALISON: It was pretty difficult to believe at the time. I couldn't understand it.

89

HELENA: I could hardly believe it myself.

ALISON: Afterwards, it wasn't quite so difficult. You used to say some pretty harsh things about him. Not that I was sorry to hear them—they were rather comforting then. But you even shocked me sometimes.

HELENA: I suppose I was a little over-emphatic. There doesn't seem much point in trying to explain everything, does there?

ALISON: Not really.

HELENA: Do you know—I have discovered what is wrong with Jimmy? It's very simple really. He was born out of his time.

ALISON: Yes. I know.

HELENA: There's no place for people like that any longer—in sex, or politics, or anything. That's why he's so futile. Sometimes, when I listen to him, I feel he thinks he's still in the middle of the French Revolution. And that's where he ought to be, of course. He doesn't know where he is, or where he's going. He'll never do anything, and he'll never amount to anything.

ALISON: I suppose he's what you'd call an Eminent Victorian. Slightly comic—in a way. . . . We seem to have had this conversation before.

HELENA: Yes, I remember everything you said about him. It horrified me. I couldn't believe that you could have married someone like that. Alison—it's all over between Jimmy and me. I can see it now. I've got to get out. No—listen to me. When I saw you standing there tonight, I knew that it was all utterly wrong. That I didn't believe in any of this, and not Jimmy or anyone could make me believe otherwise. (*Rising.*) How could I have ever thought I could get away with it! He wants one world and I want another, and lying in that bed won't ever change it! I believe in good and evil, and I don't have to apologise for that. It's quite a modern, scientific belief now, so they tell me. And, by everything I have ever believed in, or wanted, what I have been doing is wrong and evil.

ALISON: Helena—you're not going to leave him?

HELENA: Yes, I am. (*Before Alison can interrupt, she goes on.*) Oh, I'm not stepping aside to let you come back. You can do what you like. Frankly, I think you'd be a fool—but that's your own business. I think I've given you enough advice.

ALISON: But he—he'll have no one.

HELENA: Oh, my dear, he'll find somebody. He'll probably hold court here like one of the Renaissance popes. Oh, I know I'm throwing the book of rules at you, as you call it, but, believe me, you're never going to be happy without it. I tried throwing it away all these months, but I know now it just doesn't work. When you came in at that door, ill and tired and hurt, it was all over for me. You see—I didn't know about the baby. It was such a shock. It's like a judgment on us.

ALISON: You saw me, and I had to tell you what had happened. I lost the child. It's a simple fact. There is no judgment, there's no blame——

HELENA: Maybe not. But I feel it just the same.

ALISON: But don't you see? It isn't logical!

HELENA: No, it isn't. (*Calmly.*) But I know it's right.
The trumpet gets louder.

ALISON: Helena, (*going to her*) you mustn't leave him. He needs you, I know he needs you——

HELENA: Do you think so?

ALISON: Maybe you're not the right one for him—we're neither of us right——

HELENA: (*moving upstage*). Oh, why doesn't he stop that damned noise!

ALISON: He wants something quite different from us. What it is exactly I don't know—a kind of cross between a mother and a Greek courtesan, a henchwoman, a mixture of Cleopatra and Boswell. But give him a little longer——

HELENA: (*wrenching the door open*). Please! Will you stop that! I can't think!

There is a slight pause, and the trumpet goes on. She puts her hands to her head.

Jimmy, for God's sake!

It stops.

Jimmy, I want to speak to you.

JIMMY: *(off)*. Is your friend still with you?

HELENA: Oh, don't be an idiot, and come in here!
She moves down L.

ALISON: *(rising)*. He doesn't want to see me.

HELENA: Stay where you are, and don't be silly. I'm sorry. It won't be very pleasant, but I've made up my mind to go, and I've got to tell him now.
Enter Jimmy.

JIMMY: Is this another of your dark plots? *(He looks at Alison.)* Hadn't she better sit down? She looks a bit ghastly.

HELENA: I'm so sorry, dear. Would you like some more tea, or an aspirin or something?
Alison shakes her head, and sits. She can't look at either of them.
(to Jimmy, the old authority returning). It's not very surprising, is it? She's been very ill, she's——

JIMMY: *(quietly)*. You don't have to draw a diagram for me—I can see what's happened to her.

HELENA: And doesn't it mean anything to you?

JIMMY: I don't exactly relish the idea of anyone being ill, or in pain. It was my child too, you know. But *(he shrugs)* it isn't my first loss.

ALISON: *(on her breath)*. It was mine.
He glances at her, but turns back to Helena quickly.

JIMMY: What are you looking so solemn about? What's she doing here?

ALISON: I'm sorry, I'm—— *(Presses her hand over her mouth.)*
Helena crosses to Jimmy C., and grasps his hand.

HELENA: Don't please. Can't you see the condition she's in? She's done nothing, she's said nothing, none of it's her fault.
He takes his hand away, and moves away a little downstage.

92

JIMMY: What isn't her fault?

HELENA: Jimmy—I don't want a brawl, so please——

JIMMY: Let's hear it, shall we?

HELENA: Very well. I'm going downstairs to pack my things. If I hurry, I shall just catch the 7.15 to London.

They both look at him, but he simply leans forward against the table, not looking at either of them.

This is not Alison's doing—you must understand that. It's my own decision entirely. In fact, she's just been trying to talk me out of it. It's just that suddenly, tonight, I see what I have really known all along. That you can't be happy when what you're doing is wrong, or is hurting someone else. I suppose it could never have worked, anyway, but I do love you, Jimmy. I shall never love anyone as I have loved you. (*Turns away L.*) But I can't go on. (*Passionately and sincerely.*) I can't take part—in all this suffering. I can't!

She appeals to him for some reaction, but he only looks down at the table, and nods. Helena recovers, and makes an effort to regain authority.

(*to Alison*). You probably won't feel up to making that journey again tonight, but we can fix you up at an hotel before I go. There's about half an hour. I'll just make it.

She turns up to the door, but Jimmy's voice stops her.

JIMMY: (*in a low, resigned voice*). They all want to escape from the pain of being alive. And, most of all, from love. (*Crosses to the dressing table.*) I always knew something like this would turn up—some problem, like an ill wife—and it would be too much for those delicate, hot-house feelings of yours.

He sweeps up Helena's things from the dressing table, and crosses over to the wardrobe. Outside, the church bells start ringing.

It's no good trying to fool yourself about love. You can't fall into it like a soft job, without dirtying up your hands. (*Hands her the make-up things, which she takes. He opens the wardrobe.*) It takes muscle and guts.

And if you can't bear the thought (*takes out a dress on a hanger*) of messing up your nice, clean soul, (*crossing back to her*) you'd better give up the whole idea of life, and become a saint. (*Puts the dress in her arms.*)
Because you'll never make it as a human being. It's either this world or the next.

She looks at him for a moment, and then goes out quickly. He is shaken, and he avoids Alison's eyes, crossing to the window. He rests against it, then bangs his fist against the frame.

Oh, those bells!

The shadows are growing around them. Jimmy stands, his head against the window pane. Alison is huddled forward in the armchair R. Presently, she breaks the stillness, and rises to above the table.

ALISON: I'm . . . sorry. I'll go now.

She starts to move upstage. But his voice pulls her up.

JIMMY: You never even sent any flowers to the funeral. Not—a little bunch of flowers. You had to deny me that too, didn't you?

She starts to move, but again he speaks.

The injustice of it is almost perfect! The wrong people going hungry, the wrong people being loved, the wrong people dying!

She moves to the gas stove. He turns to face her.

Was I really wrong to believe that there's a—a kind of—burning virility of mind and spirit that looks for something as powerful as itself? The heaviest, strongest creatures in this world seem to be the loneliest. Like the old bear, following his own breath in the dark forest. There's no warm pack, no herd to comfort him. That voice that cries out doesn't *have* to be a weakling's, does it?

He moves in a little.

Do you remember that first night I saw you at that grisly party? You didn't really notice me, but I was watching you all the evening. You seemed to have a wonderful relaxation of spirit. I knew that was what I

wanted. You've got to be really brawny to have that
kind of strength—the strength to relax. It was only
after we were married that I discovered that it wasn't
relaxation at all. In order to relax, you've first got to
sweat your guts out. And, as far as you were concerned,
you'd never had a hair out of place, or a bead of sweat
anywhere.

A cry escapes from her, and her fist flies to her mouth.
She moves down to below the table, leaning on it.

I may be a lost cause, but I thought if you loved me, it
needn't matter.

She is crying silently. He moves down to face her.

ALISON: It doesn't matter! I was wrong, I was wrong! I don't
want to be neutral, I don't want to be a saint. I want to
be a lost cause. I want to be corrupt and futile!

All he can do is watch her helplessly. Her voice takes on a
little strength, and rises.

Don't you understand? It's gone! It's gone! That—
that helpless human being inside my body. I thought it
was so safe, and secure in there. Nothing could take it
from me. It was mine, my responsibility. But it's lost.

She slides down against the leg of the table to the floor.

All I wanted was to die. I never knew what it was like.
I didn't know it could be like that! I was in pain, and
all I could think of was you, and what I'd lost.
(*Scarcely able to speak.*) I thought: if only—if only he
could see me now, so stupid, and ugly and ridiculous.
This is what he's been longing for me to feel. This is
what he wants to splash about in! I'm in the fire, and
I'm burning, and all I want is to die! It's cost him his
child, and any others I might have had! But what does
it matter—this is what he wanted from me!

She raises her face to him.

Don't you see! I'm in the mud at last! I'm grovelling!
I'm crawling! Oh, God——

She collapses at his feet. He stands, frozen for a moment,
then he bends down and takes her shaking body in his arms.
He shakes his head, and whispers:

JIMMY: Don't. Please don't. . . . I can't——
She gasps for her breath against him.
You're all right. You're all right now. Please, I—
I. . . . Not any more. . . .
*She relaxes suddenly. He looks down at her, full of
fatigue, and says with a kind of mocking, tender irony:*
We'll be together in our bear's cave, and our squirrel's
drey, and we'll live on honey, and nuts—lots and lots of
nuts. And we'll sing songs about ourselves—about warm
trees and snug caves, and lying in the sun. And you'll
keep those big eyes on my fur, and help me keep my
claws in order, because I'm a bit of a soppy, scruffy
sort of a bear. And I'll see that you keep that sleek,
bushy tail glistening as it should, because you're a very
beautiful squirrel, but you're none too bright either, so
we've got to be careful. There are cruel steel traps
lying about everywhere, just waiting for rather mad,
slightly satanic, and very timid little animals. Right?
Alison nods.
(*pathetically*). Poor squirrels!
ALISON: (*with the same comic emphasis*). Poor bears! *She laughs
a little. Then looks at him very tenderly, and adds very,
very softly.*) Oh, poor, poor bears!
Slides her arms around him.

CURTAIN